I would like to express my appreciation to Rosalind
Brooks for allowing me to use the pen and ink sketch,
"The Shanty," by her late husband, Robert Brooks,
to *The Register*, which published a column of my
Recollections for several years, to Warren Hansen and
Paul Chesbro for photos used in WWII section, and
to Marion Vuilleumier and the workshop for giving
me valuable advice and encouragement.

This book is dedicated with love to my husband, Bob, who made me realize how rich my childhood was, and to my children and grandchildren so they may share the memories.

Special thanks to my son, Bob Jr. for his artistic help with the cover and manuscript.

AMBERGRIS AND ARROWHEADS:

Growing up on Cape Cod
In the 1930s and 1940s   8/28/03

To Lois,
I hope you enjoy looking back
at another time
Best Wishes
Anne N. Harmon

Anne N. Harmon

North Bay Press

LIBRARY of CONGRESS CATALOG CARD NUMBER 93-84771

ISBN 0-9636949-0-1

North Bay Press
P.O. Box 93
Osterville, MA 02655

Ambergris and Arrowheads

Ambergris and arrowheads. When I was growing up on Cape Cod, I looked for both and found neither... but along the way, memories gathered.

I grew up in the small village of Osterville. My childhood spanned some of the Great Depression and all of World War II. The 1930's and '40's were a unique time in our history.

I began writing a newspaper column a few years ago, based on these memories. I heard from people who grew up at the same time in other parts of the country. I discovered that many of the memories belonged to them, too.

It seemed I was not just writing about a place, but an era.

I hope among these recollections and reflections you will find some of your own.

CONTENTS

Recollections

Ambergris and Arrowheads

Ambergris and arrowheads. I have looked for both and found neither.

I was about seven when I first heard about ambergris. I asked my mother what it was. She helped me look it up in the dictionary. We found that it was a secretion from the intestines of the sperm whale. It washed up on the shore, and was very valuable.

My friends and I started searching the shores. We didn't know just what it looked like but we knew it would make us rich if we found it. We'd also been told that it was used in making perfume.

We assumed we would know it when we found some. We poked and prodded bunches of fish-eggs and smelly bits of fish, then decided it couldn't be ambergris if it smelled so bad. After all we reasoned, if they make perfume out of it, it must smell good. So much for the reasoning powers of young children.

Although we never found ambergris, we found many other treasures on the shores of our village. We must have picked a ton of lovely lavender beach heather to take home to mothers and grandmothers over the years.

Sand glass was a rare treasure. Sometimes a beautiful blue or green piece, smooth and opaque from the washing of the sand and tides would catch our eye and our day would be made.

Shells were abundant, but perfect shells were not. Often we would race to one, thinking it was perfect, only to find on closer inspection, a chip or crack. Somehow we found our share of perfect ones.

We always went home with something wonderful, even if it wasn't ambergris.

Sometimes we would see a bottle drifting in on a wave and fantasize about a note being in it from somebody on a desert island. By the time it hit shore, we would be so caught up in our story that we would invent an imaginary note and make our plans for rescue anyway.

Driftwood was always a favorite. The smooth, soft, gray look of it intrigued us. The interesting shapes were such that they suggested an animal or exotic tree. Some pieces seemed just right for carving.

As we searched for treasures, we kept a close eye on the rocks and stones wherever our journeys took us. We knew that Indians had lived nearby. We thrilled to the thought of finding an arrowhead that had been used long ago by a real Indian.

Alas, it was not to be. I must have picked up hundreds of stones, turning them every which way trying to convince myself that I had really found one, but I never did.

I'm still looking.

Aunts, Grandmothers, and Buttons

Our village was full of "aunts" and "grandmothers" for me to visit, which I did frequently.

There was Grandma Scudder whose house was almost across from what is now the Country Store. Grandma Alley lived in back of where the condominiums are on the corner of Main Street and Blossom Avenue. Her little cottage is still there in the midst of this bustling, now modern village. Grandma Small's home was two doors after Blossom, on Main Street, coming from the village center.

Aunt Marjorie and Aunt Genevieve Leonard lived where Cazeault Roofing is now. The first house on the right on Parker Road was Aunt Ethel Hall's, then further down in Crosby Town on what is now Cockachoiset Lane was Aunt Mamie Crosby's. There were others, but these were my regular stopping places.

These ladies weren't all really my aunts and grandmothers but were related in some way, as were most of us in the village. Back then, the adults knew the exact relationships... who were first cousins twice removed, and who were fourth cousins, etc. It was amazing.

Aunt Marjorie Leonard was the recognized genealogy expert. Her niece, Judy Leonard and I were best friends and wanted to know desperately how closely we were related. It took a little doing but Aunt Marjorie traced the families back and gave us written copies to prove we were related through the Parkers a few generations back. I had that abbreviated genealogy for years.

One day when I was visiting Grandma Scudder, she invited me to look through her button box while she fixed cookies and milk. It opened a whole new world for me. I was fascinated!

She told me stories of parties to which certain dresses with a particular set of buttons had been worn. There were pewter buttons with beautiful designs, and black glass ones with colorful scenes, rubber buttons made by the Goodyear Rubber Company. That information was stamped right on the button. Mother of Pearl was also a popular one, glowing with iridescent colors. She also showed me military buttons taken from the uniforms of the men in her family who had served in the early wars.

I started a button collection. I still have many of the buttons, given to me by different aunts and grandmothers. I have forgotten many of the stories and which buttons came from whom, but I will never forget the pleasure they received from sharing their memories and the fun I had visiting each one of them, hearing their stories, and collecting the buttons... not to mention all those delicious cookies!

Before Skating Rinks

In the early 1930's and 40's the ponds in the village were surrounded mostly by woods with just a few houses. We roamed the perimeters freely. I knew somebody owned them, but at that time we had free access. It would be impossible now.

There are three ponds all in a row off Pond Street... Sam's, Joshua's, and Mike's. Each had its own function. Sam's Pond is the smallest and is what the old folks called a "bottomless pond" meaning the bottom was so muddy and soft that it was not for swimming, but it was great for fishing and skating. In skating season, we would spend most of our days there. At night it seemed like most of the village would come skating. There would be little fires burning at different spots around the pond, and people would toast hot dogs or just warm their hands and feet near them.

The fire department always checked the ponds to see if they were safe for skating. Older brothers and sisters laced and unlaced skates for younger siblings, sometimes grudgingly and hurriedly, but they did it. Hockey wasn't played much then, but one things the older ones did play was "whip." They would all join hands and race across the pond. Then the leader, at one end, would stop. As everyone came to a stop abruptly, the ones on the end would be whipped around, and sometimes several would lose their grip and go flying across the pond. It was so exciting, both for the participants and the spectators!

One man who loved skating was a Norwegian named Ole. That may not be how he spelled his name, but that's how I remember it. He was sort of a hermit, living alone in a small house near Joshua's Pond, where he generated his own electricity. When there was enough snow, he would ski into the village to do his errands. He had a very long beard, which he would hold up out of the water when he bathed in Joshua's Pond. He had an old world courtesy. I remember that one evening he waltzed with me on skates. It was wonderful. I felt like such a lady!

Joshua's Pond was where we swam. It is a big, beautiful pond with lots of springs, so it was always fresh and unusually cold, especially when we would sneak in for a dip around the end of April or the first part of May. We were swimming daily by Memorial Day. The bottom always looked black and ugly when the summer began, but after a few weeks of swimming, the black would recede, and the firm sandy bottom would be there for the rest of the season.

We skated on Joshua's sometimes, but it took longer to become safe for skating than Sam's because it was much larger and had so many springs. After a real long cold snap we would skate on it. It would rumble and make sharp cracking noises, which were pretty scary. My great-grandmother Annie Hodges told me that when she was a girl and lived near the pond, her brother would lend her some of his clothes, and they would slip out of the house after everyone was asleep and go skating. Pretty daring for the early 1870's!

Mike's was where the boys went skinny-dipping. At least that's what we were told.

Bottles

Years ago, each household had their own dumping spot. Usually it was at the rear of their property. Sometimes rubbish was deposited at a place that didn't seem to belong to anybody.

After a while it grew to be the dumping area for several families. I guess it was the forerunner of the town dump.

Private dumps were eventually fazed out but not forgotten. Most of the rubbish disintegrated but glass and china didn't. China was discarded only if it was broken, so was of no value to the people who later scoured the dumps for treasures. Only an archaeologist several hundred years from now might have an interest in those broken dishes.

The bottles were the treasures everyone sought. Before the plastic age that we live in, glass was the container of choice. Bottles became an art form.

We had several bottle dumps around the village. Our family went digging on weekends.

We were cautioned to wear heavy shoes and if we had gloves, we wore them. There was lots of broken glass, but with careful digging, we unearthed occasional beauties along with everyday bottles that were in every household, such as vanilla, bitters, apothecary, milk and jelly containers. We loved to find perfume bottles. They always smelled so good!

Our favorites were ink bottles. They came in a rainbow of colors from pale aqua to amethyst. Their shapes were intriguing. They were tall, short, round, square, but no matter what their lower half looked like, most of them had a narrow chimney for a neck. Some bottles were smooth, some rough textured. Others were bubbled, feeling like they would melt in your hand at any moment.

When our son was young and the bottle dumps that we knew, were either exhausted or on PRIVATE, private property, he made a discovery right outside our back door.

We had had a line dug for some pipe, and in the digging, my son who was helping, unearthed some broken dishes. Working carefully, he discovered two beautiful bottles, one brown and one amber. Both had the same lettering on them. It proclaimed the contents to be, Dr. Ham's Aromatic Invigorating Spirits, N.Y.

We live on a very small lot in the center of the village, so I'm sure that there are still treasures to be found.

I have a beautiful cobalt blue inkwell on my kitchen window sill and the amber Dr. Ham's bottle picking up the sunshine in the den.

I checked with an expert about the bottle once, and was told that it was quite common.

Evidently the contents must have been both aromatic and invigorating.

Churches

There were four churches in our village when I was growing up. Our Lady of the Assumption, the Catholic church, and St. Peter's Episcopal Chapel were on Wianno Ave. The Osterville Baptist Church and the Osterville Community Church were on Main Street.

Our family belonged to the Baptist church. It was a big part of our lives. I still have my Sunday School pins signifying nine years perfect attendance. (My brother had eleven.) My grandparents who lived next door to us went to the morning service at eleven every Sunday. Grandpa went early because he was the one who rang the bell calling everyone to church. Somebody rang the Community Church bells alternately with ours. As soon as Sunday school was over at 10:30, I would race up the stairs to the room where the bell rope hung. Grandpa would let me "help" him ring the bell. We would both pull it down with all our might and then let it go. It would fly up as the bell rang out. Sometimes my

9

grandfather would let me hang on to it in its upward flight, and I would be lifted off my feet about a foot into the air. I was light enough so that the bell still rang. We didn't tell anybody about my flights, especially my grandmother, who wouldn't have considered it "proper" Sunday behavior.

In those days, everyone dressed in Sunday best to go to church or Sunday school. One day, when I was in third grade, I was changing out of my clothes after church, when I noticed spots on my stomach. I had German measles. I was so glad nobody had noticed them before I had gone. I wanted my attendance to be perfect, even though you got credit for going if you were really sick. The following Thursday was my birthday. My mother had made plans for a party for me at school, but my spots were not all gone, so I couldn't go. The children in the class made birthday cards for me and ate the refreshments my mother had sent. The cards were nice but didn't really make up for a party!

What happened that evening did. Our church was having a penny auction in the vestry and I was allowed to go. That night, I got everything I bid on, and not by coincidence. Everyone there knew I'd missed school that day and said "Happy Birthday" to me in a very special way.

There was always something going on at the churches. The Community church used to show Charlie Chaplin movies in its vestry, and rummage sales were often held in the churches. Church suppers were wonderful. I used to love to go and help in the kitchen. We children were probably more bother than we were worth, but everyone was very patient with us and said how much we helped.

The Ecumenical movement didn't exist in those days, but we didn't know it. My closest friends were from churches other than mine, and though we argued about whose church was best, as we would over many things, there was no real friction. I even belonged to the Catholic church's girls club.

The churches were important in both our religious and social lives. We went on retreats, had Youth Fellowship get togethers, softball games, food sales, and progressive suppers, and of course caroling and church-sponsored sledding parties in the winter. Church life and village life were much entwined.

The church bells were always rung for joyous occasions and the one I remember the most, was the day that they were rung to celebrate the end of World War II... and I helped.

The Community Center

In 1938 or 39, I remember watching my father and a group of men work on what was to be our Community Center. It was where the Dry Swamp Academy had been, behind and to the right of the Osterville Baptist Church. The Center became a very important part of our village life.

My earliest recollections are of a man named Mr. Tattersal, who was in charge. He had a big whip that he did tricks with. It also gave him an air of authority.

The Center had an entry hall with stairs to the lower level. On the left was the basketball court. Off the court on each side were rooms used for meetings and classes. The Historical Society occupied one of those rooms for years.

I remember one class in particular that was held in the other room. It was in metal craft. We made metal bracelets and engraved them. They were more like cuffs, actually, made to resemble Wonder Woman's. When they were completed, off we went to the golf course to play Wonder Woman. Flying was simulated by jumping into the sand traps.

The office of the person running the Center was at the front of the basketball court. There was a window in it facing the entry hall so that the supervisor could see who came and went.

Downstairs in the basement room were ping-pong tables, plus the restrooms and the kitchen. The kitchen was also used as a darkroom when we had a class in film developing. What a thrill it was, developing our first pictures!

Around the corner from the ping-pong tables was a spot where there was a piano. Anybody could play it. I guess we must have played duets like "I Love Coffee-I Love Tea" at least a thousand times over the years.

Beyond the piano area was another good sized room. It was for reading and games. There were books, magazines, cards and board games. That room had doors on it, so that the noise from the wildly competitive ping-pong tournaments could be somewhat muffled. We played tournaments with other villages and even other towns. I remember competing against a team from Falmouth and also going to Buzzards Bay to play for our town.

My favorite thing in the whole world was basketball. We played every chance we had. Even when we were small, the bigger kids would allow us a shot now and then, when they were tired or when it was between games. Then we would get our chance. As we grew older we played more and more. We played boys' basketball and upon entering junior high, we girls who had competed with the boys at the Center, found the girls rules (half-court, one bounce) very tame and confining.

Throughout my youth, the Center was my home away from home. In my teens, I'd spend the evening at the Center and allow myself two minutes to make it home by curfew. I would race out the door, cut through in back of the Baptist church and Central Garage, which was next to it, and race for home.

I usually made it.

Ghosts

Some mornings I walk with ghosts.

Usually I walk with my sister-in-law, but those mornings when she doesn't come, I walk with my dog and meet with ghosts from the past.

Having lived in this village all my life and been raised on the oral history of my family, some of whom had lived here in the seventeen hundreds, I find few spots where I have no ghostly reminders.

I usually walk up town as we say in this village, meaning to the center where the stores are. I can visualize the stores and houses that used to be on the street years ago.

Would you believe we had a First National Store and an A & P two doors apart? There were several houses dotted among the stores. Some are now businesses, some have been moved or torn down, or like the former library, been incorporated into another building.

I look at the remaining portion of the library and see the librarian, Miss Hinckley, admonishing me to wash my hands before touching any of the books. In spite of her sternness, she appreciated and nurtured my love of reading. I wander along and there is Grandma Scudder inviting me in for cookies and to look through her button box.

It's not only the ghosts of people who approach me, it's a favorite tree that asks me to touch it like I used to as a child, when I'd try to reach all the way around its trunk. When nobody's looking, I try to reach around now. Its bark is like an elephant's hide. I still can't reach all the way around it. It seems I'm not the only one who has added girth through the years.

I walk down to the old boat shop, peeking in the door of the large workroom. The wonderful smell of wood being planed draws me. Is it real, or from the past when I would slip in and stand for hours watching the men plane the boards for the skiffs and dories they were building? I'd hold the long curly cues of planed wood against my head for curls and the men would take time to look up and laugh, before busying themselves again.

Sometimes I would ask to borrow a skiff to go out on the bay fishing. If there was one not being used, I'd be given permission to row out for an hour or two.

As I walked past the school, I see the boys of long ago springs watching the outdoor thermometer, and hear them beg Miss Sherman, the principal to be allowed to play ball at recess. She won't budge. No baseball until the thermometer reaches fifty.

I remember many things about the school, but something pops into my head this morning that I haven't thought about for years. Perhaps it's the current economic times that brings it to mind.

I see myself in school during the depression. We had little or nothing in the way of spare cash. Small bottles of milk were sold to the children each morning. It cost five cents a week for regular milk and ten for chocolate. I couldn't buy either.

The ghost that I see this morning is Mr. Coleman who was the janitor at the time. He bought my milk every week, not regular, but chocolate. The only stipulation was that I would not say anything.

All the ghosts in the village are not friendly. We have our share of meanies; those who just plain never liked kids and some who were born and died mean. When I walk by them now, I don't quake in my boots as I did then. Well, perhaps I still walk a little faster as I go by.

When I returned from my walk, my husband saw the dog and me coming into the yard.

"You walked alone today," he said.

I smiled to myself.

"Well, sort of."

The Golf Course

The golf course winds around the southwest side of the village. All kinds of dwellings border it, from modest cottages to large estates. It is the same today as it was when I was growing up, except I don't play there anymore.

It is a private, exclusive club. When I was a child, the villagers didn't have memberships there. It was mainly for the summer people. That has changed some over the years.

To the children of the village, it was a playground, a giant, wonderful playground.

We had unofficial year-round memberships. It included ponds that we swam in, others that we skated on.

Some of its hills provided the best sliding in the village. They still do.

We learned early not to abuse it, not to interfere with the golfers, and especially not to run afoul of the pro.

From where I lived, it was much easier to cut across the course to do my paper route and to shortcut in another direction to make it to the boat yard long before my brother could get there by bike, taking the road.

We spent hours of hunting lost golf balls. We'd polish them at the tees, keep the old gouged ones for our own golf games, and sell the others. We found them in the rough, in the woods, in the ponds and on the shore of North Bay.

There was an army of us on the lookout for them most of the time.

The sand traps provided us with as much fun and adventure as they gave aggravation to the golfers. We used them as foxholes during the war, and to bury ourselves. Strapping contraptions on our arms, and jumping into the traps, we foreshadowed the art of hang gliding.

We were master disappearing artists. When a group of golfers were headed our way, we would disappear like shadows into the woods or tall grass that edged the fairway. We carefully watched as they played past us, keeping an eye on each ball.

If a golfer shot into the woods or rough, we would mark it with precision and wait. If the golfers and their caddies gave up on it and moved on, we all rose up like Apaches from the desert and raced for the location. There was a lot of competition among us, but whoever found the ball was congratulated, because in the end, what counted, was that we had outwitted the players.

Most of us had an old club or two and could make up a pretty good set for our pick-up games. We knew the routine of the ground crews and when the course was liable to be free, so we played when the opportunity presented itself.

It was a wonderful place. Wide open spaces, woods to play in, the bay with the boats coming and going in summer, the hills for sliding in the winter, the thrill of the hunt, the sharing of money made for treats. We harmed nothing and I'm sure now that the golf pro knew all about our activities but let it go.

Maybe it was because he had always loved golf courses, too. I mean after all, he had to know all the tricks to become the pro.

Grandma Takes a Stand

Many years ago there were sometimes less than cordial feelings between some of the summer residents and the village people, but as a whole, both the adult summer and village population managed to keep on the veneer of civilization.

16

Not so the children.

Fights and taunts between these two groups were a common occurrence. Usually it was over the fair sex. Either a village boy was going out with a summer girl or summer boy was dating village girls. Neither was acceptable. That didn't stop it from happening of course. If a village couple didn't break up in the summer to accommodate a summer romance, that couple was considered ready to tie the knot!

There were no serious incidents that I can recall, just the usual joustings of the adolescent males.

My grandmother's story, however, was different. It cut to the very heart of a major problem. The shores of the village had always been accessible to everyone, but as the wealthier people discovered our village and purchased the shorefront, things changed. Fences went up, docks were built and gradually resentments were sparked.

We were always taught that below the high water mark was public domain and so it remained for years. Now I think that has changed in some quarters but that was after my grandmother's time.

The tale I am about to tell, happened before I was born, so I can't testify to the truth of it, but having known my grandmother, I believe every word.

Grandma Hodges was born off Cape. My grandfather met her while working in Taunton. She came from a well-to-do family. I always had the feeling that she thought she married below her station. She was a LADY. She was also what my great grandmother called a "tartar."

I think until this particular incident happened, she felt more sympathy with the summer people than she did with the villagers. Her sympathy changed one lovely Sunday.

Grandma had decided to accompany my grandfather fishing. She rarely did this but the beauty of the day overcame her reservations. During the early afternoon, while fishing in the waters in

17

front of Wianno, Grandma asked Grandpa to pull into shore so that she could get out and stretch her legs.

Grandpa beached the skiff. Grandma walked up and down the beach for a few minutes. Suddenly, down over the banking, came the woman who owned the house above. She flew at Grandma like an angry hornet.

"You can't stay on my beach. You will have to leave at once. I am having guests and we will be having lunch down here."

Grandma drew herself up into her most haughty pose.

"I beg your pardon. I am not on your beach. If you will take note of the debris behind you, you will see where the high water mark is. Your beach starts there, and I have every intention of remaining where I am for as long as I wish."

The lady sputtered a while longer and then returned to the house, sending her husband down. He tried a different tactic. He was most apologetic for his wife's behavior and tried to charm Grandma off the beach.

It didn't work.

"Will," called Grandma, "bring the barrel to me, please."

Grandpa brought the barrel which was in the skiff. It was used to put fish in, but at the moment Grandma didn't care how badly it smelled. She was embarked on a mission. She turned the barrel over, placed it near the high water mark, and sat on it.

"Will," she directed, "I will be remaining here for a while. Please pick me up before high tide."

Will took her meaning, and smiled. His wife was acting like a stubborn Cape Codder.

"I'll be back before tide change, Mother."

Grandpa came back near sunset and just before the water reached the high tide mark. He put the barrel in the skiff and assisted Grandma, who graciously took his arm. Although she said afterward she felt stiff as a board, she wouldn't let those people peeking out of the windows of the big house know it.

After they had rowed out a ways, Grandma sighed, and relaxed, rubbing a few sore spots.

"That was the longest afternoon of my life, Will, but it was worth it. I guess we showed them a thing or two."

Grandpa grinned and patted her knee. "You certainly did, Mother, you certainly did."

Grandma was finally becoming a villager.

Hillside Cemetery

Cemeteries may not seem like an upbeat subject, but our cemetery on Old Mill Road is a big part of our village history. I'm sure that a book could be written on this subject, but I just want to recall a few memories.

When I was young, I always went with my mother on Memorial Day to plant flowers at the graves of some of our ancestors. At my early age, it seemed such a gaily decorated place. There were flowers and flags everywhere. A holiday atmosphere pervaded everything. As the years passed and our annual pilgrimage continued, I became more aware of the solemnity of Memorial Day. For the first time I noticed that most people there kept their voices lowered, and although pleasantries were exchanged, everything was subdued. Families were remembering.

On the last school day before Memorial Day, we had our school parade, exercises at the monument uptown and then we marched to the cemetery to put flowers on the veterans' graves, which were specially marked.

Although we took this duty fairly seriously, I have to admit that our thoughts kept drifting to going swimming afterwards. Our school day was over as soon as we laid the flowers.

We managed to contain our exuberance until we cleared the cemetery grounds, but then a holiday spirit took over.

I grew up with pleasant feelings about Hillside and would occasionally go there and walk around reading the stones. There is one with a story about a young sailor lost at sea.

I loved to look at our family's stones. I hadn't known my great-great grandparents, Sarah and Nathan West, but I had heard many stories about them from their daughter, Annie, my great grandmother. She also told me stories about her brothers and sisters. Mostly she told me about her husband, Frank Hodges. She married him when she was sixteen. She had been told that he would die young because of heart problems, but she told me triumphantly, "I kept him almost forty years."

There are hundreds of stories at Hillside. You can read, etched in the old stones, stories of heartbreak, of several children in a family dying the same year in a diphtheria epidemic, of men lost at sea, of women dying in childbirth, of young men going off to war, and not returning. Among those stories of heartbreak, you will also see stories of long lives lived to the fullest, families overcoming losses, continuing on, living their lives and building our village.

Hurricanes

Everyone has a story to tell about Hurricane Bob, which hit Cape Cod on August 19, 1991, but I would like to recollect the hurricane of 1944.

Carol... Edna... Gloria... they all wreaked havoc in their own way but the day after Hurricane Bob, as I walked around our village I was eleven years old again.

It looked like 1944, like worn torn countries we'd been seeing on the news at the movies.

Hurricane Bob swept through much quicker than the '44 hurricane. That one seemed to last forever in my young mind. It also brought with it what we called a tidal wave in those days.

The morning after was sunny and beautiful. The devastation was exciting and ugly at the same time.

The first thing I saw when I opened our front door was a long time friend, a towering mulberry tree strewn across my grandparents drive and into the street, lying along with several others.

I had first climbed into the low crotch of that tree when I was four. I spent many hours in its branches in the intervening years watching for friends to arrive, sulking when confined to the yard for some misdemeanor, reading an Oz book or just watching the comings and goings of folks in the village.

I remember patting its massive trunk the day after the hurricane and then moving on. There was too much ahead to stop and stay then. I would cry over my tree later. The whole village seemed broken in pieces. The world was topsy-turvy.

Trees were uprooted everywhere, roads impassable. The golf course near my home was strewn with boats of all shapes and sizes. It was an astonishing sight.

The woods in the middle of the course had so many uprooted trees that we could see through to the other side for the first time. The huge caves created by the roots being torn up became our forts and foxholes for the remainder of World War II.

Our mood alternated between excitement, amazement, and sadness.

As morning progressed, we realized along with the adults, that no one was going to be able to remove all the trees blocking the roads. It would be difficult to get to the areas where there were summer people who had not left Labor Day weekend. People headed to different places along the shores to see what they could do.

My friend and I climbed over tree trunks on a two-mile trek to the end of Sea View Avenue near what's known as the Cut.

There we found members of a family who were happy to see us even if we were kids. They said they felt isolated and cut off and had no idea what to do. We told them everything we had seen.

They had enough in the house to get by until adult help could arrive, but in the meantime, they wrote telegrams to their family off Cape. They gave us money to send them off, thanked us for coming, and insisted we keep the change.

We rushed back to the newsstand in the village, feeling important with our news that everyone out there was safe. We were also puffed up with the responsibility for sending the telegrams. The best part, however, was the five dollars that was ours to split when the transaction was completed.

Later, we went down to check on Johnny Crosby's oyster shanty, which perched on the edge of the bay near the Oyster Harbors Bridge. There it was, as good as new. Before the storm, Mr. Crosby had removed small items, nailed down larger ones, opened all windows and doors and left the hurricane a way to blow through. This worked for him through every hurricane. Other shanties that were all boarded up, floated away.

Every once in a while when the shanty got pretty messy, I recall Mr. Crosby saying, "We need a good blow to clean this place out."

Many homes and cottages at the beaches were beyond repair. One that was to make a lasting impact on our village was the Dowse property at what is now Dowses beach. The house took a fatal blow. It stood empty for a while after the hurricane, before the property was given to the village for a residential beach.

Before the house was torn down, we used it freely, sunbathing on the huge porch or riding up and down in the dumb waiter.

In the aftermath of the '44 hurricane, it seemed like the Cape and its villages would never be the same and it wasn't. Some things were changed forever, but the scars faded and the villages healed, and they will again after Hurricane Bob.

I spent many happy hours in this tree before it was lost in the 1944 hurricane.

Ice Cream

Can you remember before Howard Johnsons had 28 flavors, before the ice cream man existed, back to when ice cream had to be eaten within the hour because there was no way to keep it frozen? I can.

There were five flavors of ice cream then: chocolate, vanilla, coffee, strawberry, and frozen pudding, plus orange sherbet. There were also popcicles, fugicles, hoodsies, and sometimes pushups.

The newsstand and drugstore both had soda fountains. The Fruit Store always had cones and the other aforementioned items.

One scoop of ice cream was a nickel, two, a dime and if you really wanted to show off, you could get a three scooper for fifteen cents. That was rare because we figured out early on, that it made more economic sense to get three cones, instead of three scoops on just one cone. However that decision didn't come up often because we usually didn't have fifteen cents.

On a poor day, which came fairly often, a friend and I would have a hard time scaring up a nickel. On those days we opted for a popcicle to split, if we could agree on the flavor.

Mr. Kalas who owned the Fruit Store was always generous to us with his scoops. He also tolerated our indecision about what flavor we would get. He just didn't open up the ice cream compartments until he was certain we had made up our minds.

Remember when you were in such a hurry to bite into that cone that you forgot the dreaded "ice cream headache?" Oh, the pain! It seemed like the whole front of your face was going to explode. The only thing that would stop it was time or a drink of water. Since we were usually outside with our cones and not allowed inside anyway as long as we were eating one, we were stuck with the headache. It probably lasted only a few seconds, but it seemed like forever. Meanwhile, our ice cream was melting.

The driver who delivered the ice cream to the stores in the village both fascinated and repelled us. We were happy to see him come into the village but hated the first thing he did when he parked in front of the Fruit Store.

He always had a wad of chewing tobacco stuffed in his cheek, and on arriving, he would spit tobacco juice. It wouldn't have been so bad if he'd just spit it on the road, but he had a thing about trying to reach the island where the flagpole is now. He'd lean out of the truck and let fly. It was something to see! Although it was stomach-churning to think about, we couldn't help being fascinated enough to watch it arc over the road in its flight.

If my grandmother who lived next to the fruit store happened to be out in her yard, she would announce in a loud disapproving tone, "Filthy habit!"

The driver never gave a sign that he heard, though of course he did, along with everyone else in the neighborhood.

One of the highlights of my childhood came a day or two after the '44 hurricane. The power was off for days. When Mr. Kalas realized that it wouldn't be coming back on in time to save the huge opened containers of ice cream, he gave it to all us kids in the neighborhood.

What a treat! For once in our childhood, we had more ice cream than we could possibly consume.

So what it if was a little soft? So what if some of it was frozen pudding? We still felt like we'd died and gone to heaven!

The Island

The other day, I stopped to look at the Honor Roll for our villages' veterans of the Civil War, Mexican War and World War One. It is located on the little island where the flag flies each day, across from the Country Store on Main Street.

Back in the early 1900's the hay scale, which was a huge scale the farmers would drive their wagons of hay onto, to be weighed, was in the approximate location where the island is now. Over the years it gradually evolved into the shape of an elongated teardrop.

The flag pole was put there, as well as the permanent Honor Roll for the veterans. Before and during World War II, Memorial Day and Armistice Day services were held at the island. It was also a favorite place to play.

There were shrubs along the edges of it, behind which we used to hide while playing tricks on people. One favorite trick was giving strangers wrong directions. Often while we were going in or out of the Osterville Fruit Store (now the Osterville Country Store) someone in a car would stop and ask for directions. We'd send them down Parker Road to West Bay Road, then left to Wianno Ave, then left on Wianno, which would bring them back to their starting point. Sometimes it worked and sometimes it didn't but we would hide behind the shrubs, giggle and have a good time either way.

The other trick, which has been a favorite of everyone over the years, was putting a pocketbook on the side of the road and hoping someone would spot it, stop their car and come back. Before they could back up, we would have pulled the pocketbook to us by the attached string and by the time they realized they had been fooled, we would be hiding safely in the shrubs. Even if we got caught, most people were nice about it, more concerned with our being careful not

26

to get hurt by cars. Some even suggested a better way of doing the trick.

In later years, the town shortened the island to its present shape to make it easier for traffic, but I think it lost something in the transition. Some people from out of the town think it's a rotary which can really lead to confusion on a summer's day. I wonder if they ever had a traffic jam around the hay scales?

Kitchen Tables

In our living room is a beautiful drop-leaf mahogany table. It wasn't always beautiful. For part of its life it was an old kitchen table. Under one edge you can feel the roughness where a meat-grinder had been attached many times. My husband grew up around it. He remembers his grandmother having him tighten the grinder for her as she prepared to make relish or mincemeat. His most vivid memory of it from his childhood is not his fondest. The family doctor used it as an operating table to take my husband's tonsils out.

The small upstairs apartment in my great-grandmother's house where I spent my childhood had a kitchen so small that the table took up more than half the floor space. We used it for a lot more than meals. Most of the food preparation was done on it. My brother and I did our homework there. It became an ironing board when the old scorched sheet was thrown over a thick towel.

Saturdays around that table were best for it was baking day. Every Saturday morning my mother would take out her large, square enamel board, which was a little smaller than the table top. She would dust it with flour and begin to make pies, cakes, tarts, and Parker House rolls. With the scraps of pie crust, I was allowed to make cinnamon rolls.

Evenings after supper, we would sit around the table to talk, argue, play cards, or board games.

Usually the table was covered with oil cloth. It was colorful and above all, durable. A little wiping after each assault and it seemed good as new. Glue from making model airplanes on it would sometimes cause a problem and cutting on it could do it in, but all things considered, oil cloth was great.

I remember the table being painted several times in my childhood. Each time it was done, the writings indented in the wood where my brother and I bore down hard doing our homework, stood out with clarity.

One time, my father decided that he wanted to "brighten up the place." He certainly did! He painted the table with Chinese red enamel and put decals on each corner and in the center. The decals pictured a man with a big sombrero sitting against a cactus, having a siesta. It was not a work of art.

However, on Saturday mornings, I hardly noticed. Only the man on each corner showed. I don't know how these men could take a siesta with the wonderful smell of all those cakes, pies, cookies, tarts, and of course my special cinnamon rolls.

When I dust the table in our living room and feel the roughness, I think of my husband having his tonsils out on it, while probably at the same time my old table was painted Chinese red with a bunch of men with sombreros taking a siesta under a cactus.

Laundry

Gone are the clothes drying on radiators. Gone are most of the radiators. Baseboard heat just doesn't make it as a clothes dryer. Even small socks slip off. Clotheslines are now passe. In most developments on the Cape, they are not allowed, except when enclosed. Clothes hanging out is evidently considered visual pollution by some.

When we were growing up, everything was hung out year round. If the laundry was caught out in the rain, it usually stayed there until nature provided some sun. If some items were absolutely necessary, they were brought in to dry close to or on the stove (no radiators in our old house). Hanging out and bringing in the laundry was sometimes fun and sometimes not, but it was certainly more interesting and complex than throwing it into the dryer.

Just tracking down enough clothespins was a challenge each washday. Clothespins seem to disappear out of the laundry baskets between times. Whether they were the old fashioned pins or the new-fangled spring ones, they had numerous uses as giant paper clips, building logs, airplanes, or stick figure people.

For a while, we had a clothespin bag that hung on the line, but it would slide back and forth and in a wind the pins would be tossed from one end of the clothes-yard to the other. We kids would pick them up and put them on the clean wet clothes, leaving dirt on everything they touched.

In the cold weather, the wash would blow and snap in the wind but then when the breeze died everything would freeze on the line. We'd take in the laundry basket with few things in it. Most pieces were spread on top frozen stiff. Gradually they'd thaw enough to be spread around the house to finish drying.

The best part of hanging clothes out of doors was the wonderful smell they had when they were brought in after a brisk sunny day. It can't be duplicated. Several companies have tried with laundry products, but they don't even come close.

I have to admit that the modern washer and dryers are efficient and I certainly don't miss the all day chore with the old wringer washing machine and the clothes-yard, but I do miss that wonderful outdoorsy smell.

Once in a while on a sunny spring day when I bring the dog in from her yard, she jumps in my lap. For an instant she smells just like the fresh laundry from my clothesline days.

The Library

The library used to be almost diagonally across from our house. You can see part of it still, as part of the House and Garden Shop on Main Street. It's the square chunk of building jutting out on the left as you face the shop. It seems like such a little building, but what a big part of our lives it was!

I remember my library card number was thirty-three. My mother's was two. They were both well used. When I go into our library now, I am overwhelmed by the enormous number of books, but growing up, I knew every book in the library, and had read most of them. That is to say, I read the ones Miss Katherine Hinckley, our librarian, felt were "suitable." Talk about censorship! Miss Hinckley had no qualms whatsoever about censoring our reading material. She certainly encouraged us to read, but steered us gently and sometimes not so gently to the materials she felt were appropriate for our age and sex. She also checked our hands to make sure they were clean before we could touch anything.

Many were the times my mother took books out for me that Miss Hinckley refused to let me borrow. I was very well read, and was used to reading books far beyond what was designated for my age. My mother encouraged me to read whatever I wanted, within reason. She knew there was nothing in Miss Hinckley's domain that would harm me.

As I grew older, I sometimes found words in magazines which were not in our home dictionary so I'd go to the library to look them up in the huge dictionary there. If Miss Hinckley had seen some of the words I looked up, I'm sure she would have fainted, and once recovered, given me a cold stare and a hot lecture.

I remember our library as a wonderful place to go.

There were three rooms. The main room where the librarian's desk was, held the adult books, and it seemed rather dark in the aisles. It was dimly lit, as I remember, or maybe I had that feeling because the shelves were so tall. The children's room was bright and cheerful, with bookshelves around the room. The center was left open for a table and chairs.

The third room was off the main room. It was the adults reading room. There was a long conference type table and several heavy chairs. There was a picture of George Washington on the wall. The portrait is now at the Osterville Historical Society building.

Children were not allowed in the reading room. As a matter of fact I can only remember seeing one or two grown people in it, ever. I used to go in it at times when my mother cleaned the library. Even then I spoke in a whisper.

Miss Hinckley loved the library, although she was undoubtedly somewhat of a tyrant in her library domain. However she instilled a love and respect for it in all of us. We knew it was a privilege to be able to take out the books and were taught to be careful of them. To this day, I can't throw a book in the trash even if it's falling apart.

Reading has always been one of life's greatest pleasures to me, and it all started back in that chunky building that still lives in a small way, physically, and a much larger way in our memories.

Penny Candy

When our children were young, we used to take them to the country store for penny candy. Only it really wasn't penny candy as we had known it. It was a lot more expensive, some items costing as much as five cents. Of course, in this era of forty and fifty cent candy bars, a nickel doesn't seem like much.

When I was young we used to get a small bag full of candy for a nickel if we bought wisely and happened to like the low-priced items. Besides, even if you didn't like them, somebody did, so they were usually good for a trade of some sort.

We had a regular system when making our purchases. First we bought our very favorites. (Mine was bolsters.) Then we bought something that was five for a penny, such as licorice babies. Lastly, we wanted something we really enjoyed that would also last a long time. This particular decision usually took a while. There were so many candies that fell into that particular category, such as jawbreakers and root beer barrels.

We had to be sure what we wanted before we touched it, because the rule in the store was, that if we handled it we had to buy it. That was probably because although some of it was wrapped, most of it wasn't. The rule was a fair one considering the griminess of some of the hands.

The selection seemed enormous to us. We spent as much time deciding what we were going to get as we did consuming what we'd bought. Most of this decision making was done before we ever went into the store. It was half the fun. We changed our minds a dozen times before we went in and at least once or twice while we were waiting our turn.

If we were considered trustworthy and old enough to count, sometimes we would be allowed to fill our own bags. This was a special privilege, not to be taken lightly. The first time it happened, it was important enough to be mentioned at the supper table. One day when I had taken my open bag up for inspection, I had counted out more items than I said. The extra piece was removed and something was said to the effect that anyone can make a mistake. I was totally embarrassed and was extremely careful from then on. I knew that the real message had been that anyone could make a mistake ONCE.

After buying the candy, we'd find a relatively clean spot and dump out the contents, line up the candy, put back into the bag the ones we weren't willing to trade. Then we'd look at what everyone else had. Sometimes we kept every piece we had bought, but more often somebody else's looked better to us by then and we'd trade. A nickel bag of penny candy could be parlayed into a whole morning's fun.

Let's see, shall I get Mary Janes, black or red licorice, caramels, wax false teeth or giant wax lips. No, maybe I'll get spearmint leaves, or Squirrels or Orange Slices or...

I can't decide. You go first.

Phoebe's

Homelessness has become one of the foremost issues of today. As I was reading an article about it the other day, I was reminded of all the people I knew as a child who would have been homeless in this day and age.

In those days, many people ran boarding houses. Others took in perhaps just one boarder. Some rented rooms and their roomers ate elsewhere. There were as many different kinds of arrangements as there were people.

Some homes housed three or four generations. If girls remained unmarried, they usually stayed in their ancestral home or traveled around to relatives to help with new babies or care for the ill or elderly. Boys went off Cape to work if they didn't go to sea or have a job in the village, but even the boys stayed at home when they became men, if they were unmarried.

If there were personal reasons why a man couldn't or didn't want to live at home, he roomed out.

In the summer, there would be an influx of workers for the clubs, lodges and hotels, but most of them, such as the Wianno Club and East Bay Lodge, provided live-in accommodations for their help.

There were always single, unattached men who had no families. Some had steady jobs and some didn't, just doing odd jobs. But one thing they usually all had was a place to stay. Unless you were a really "bad apple" somebody would rent you a room.

The boarding house that I remember the best was Phoebe Ford's. It was located on the right at the bottom of the big hill on Bay Street.

When I was very young, I used to deliver papers there so I was allowed in. I loved going into the kitchen. It always smelled so good. Mrs. Ford didn't have time to visit with children but she tolerated me. It was a fascinating place to a child. Somebody was always coming or going. The house was big and rambling and a little ramshackled, with outbuildings staggered in different directions. An assortment of chickens and animals populated the yard. Fresh laundry snapped on the lines.

Mrs. Ford was usually shooing somebody, either away from a cooking pot or out into the yard or out of a room she was cleaning. She was in perpetual motion. It seemed that she always had an apron on and a long-handled spoon in her hand.

The men who boarded with her had clean beds and wonderful food. Her baked beans were legendary. My great-grandmother sent me down each Saturday afternoon about four o'clock to get a half pint of Phoebe's baked beans for her supper. I think they cost a dime.

The days of that kind of boarding house have gone forever. The regulations for how many bedrooms per bath, the kind of cooking utensils used, sprinkler systems, etc., would make it impossible to have them now, but they certainly served a useful purpose then and benefitted the village.

Boarding houses, and rooming houses sort of faded away with the coming of motels and zoning.

Ah, progress!

Radio

Radio was a very intimate part of our youth. Although we didn't have walkmans or boomboxes, we were never far from a radio.

When we watch old movies today, they quite often depict a family gathered around the radio listening to some momentous happening. We did that, too, but what we mainly listened to wasn't momentous at all, but it sure was exciting to us. *Jack Armstrong, The All American Boy, Tom Mix, The Lone Ranger, The Green Hornet, Sergeant Preston of the Yukon.* There were dozens more. They were the adventure programs that brought us home at dusk more often than hunger did.

Our mothers and grandmothers held the radio captive during the day while they cooked, cleaned, mended, and did all the other chores allotted them. The radio, in turn, held them captivated, punctuating their long days with romance, intrigue, heroism and quite often, chicanery.

The expression, "Soap Operas" came from those programs because most of the sponsors were soap companies.

I would slip into my great-grandmother's kitchen while she was listening to Oxydol's own *Ma Perkins*. Grandma would put her finger to her lips and pass me a treat which kept me quiet until whatever crisis was happening was resolved or put off until the next day. Other favorites were, *One Man's Family, Stella Dallas, and Mary Noble, Back Stage Wife.*

One program that was sponsored by Ivory Soap puzzled me. I was only about six at the time and had no knowledge of fractions. The announcer would tout the soap by saying "ninety-nine and forty-four one hundredths percent pure." I knew those two figures equalled much more than one hundred, but as it didn't seem strange to any of the grownups, I kept quiet. Thank goodness. Imagine if my big brother had found that one out. I'd have never heard the end of it!

Late on Sunday afternoon, we would all drift toward our homes to listen to *The Shadow*. I think that program was an all-time favorite.

"Who knows what evil lurks in the hearts of men? The Shadow knows!" Then a terrible laugh would emanate from the radio, sending chills down our spines and making us very happy that we were not the "bad guys," who didn't stand a chance against our hero.

As the years went by and battery radios were introduced, men working outside would tune in the ballgames on their portables.

The batteries in those days didn't last long, but even in their last throes, with a friendly tap or shake, the radio might be cajoled into "just one more inning."

Radio was never as confining as TV is. When we gathered in the living room to listen, I can remember my dad and brother working on model airplanes, my mother reading, knitting, and admonishing me about homework.

When our children were young, we would say, "If you want to watch Disney later, you'd better get your homework done."

Our parents used to say to us, "You'd better get your homework done if you want to listen to *Jack Benny*, or was it *Fibber McGee and Molly*, *Inner Sanctum*, or *I Love a Mystery*?

Television may be king now but radio is still there, informing me, entertaining me, soothing me, letting me be free.

"Hi-ho Silver, away!"

Relatives

When I was growing up, it was hard to find somebody in the village that I wasn't related to.

In our society today, there are few extended families living in the same place. A few years ago when our daughter was in nursing school, families were being discussed in class. Our daughter was the only one to have an extended family. The rest of the class couldn't imagine having grandparents, aunts, uncles, cousins, not to mention great-grandparents, all living in the same village.

As far back as I can remember, most of the adults knew whose cousin was once, twice or three times removed. One would say to me, "You must be Adenia's daughter. You look just like her. You can certainly tell you're a Hodges."

I wasn't. I was a Clarke, but because my father came from out of town (Hyannis) that didn't count. Sometimes whoever was trying to identify me, would skip a generation and declare I was the spitting image of my great-grandmother, Annie West Hodges.

"I can always tell a West," this particular person would say.

Sometimes they would go on to say how they were related to me.

"I'm your great-aunt Ethel's own cousin on her mother's side."

All this identification didn't particularly interest me at the time, especially if I was on my way to something important, like swimming, or going to a friend's house, but I was always polite because we were related, and if I had been otherwise, word would have gotten home before I did.

Of course as in most things, this situation had both advantages and disadvantages. On the plus side, there were many aunts, cousins, and grandmas to visit for cookies and milk. On the negative side, I couldn't get away with much. Any undesirable behavior was reported to my great-grandmother, grandmother, or mother with amazing speed and relish.

I was a tomboy and a wanderer. My mother sympathized and gave me a great deal of freedom, for those days. She was constantly being warned by a few that I would come to no good if I didn't conform to a more lady-like lifestyle. She thanked them for their concern and I went on my merry way. However I did not go entirely unencumbered. She gave me something to carry with me and expected me to take it to heart. It was this rhyme:

"I never can hide myself from me

38

I see what others can never see
I know what others can never know
I have to live with myself, and so
Whatever happens I want to be
Self-respecting and conscience free."
My mother was a smart lady. It worked most of the time.

Recycling

Lately, recycling is being treated as a brand new concept. It isn't. Years ago everyone recycled.

I'm not sure whether we recycled everything because we couldn't afford to buy new, or whether it was the Yankee in us that reminded us to "Waste not-want not." However, whatever the reason, nothing was thrown out that could possibly be used in some way. This went beyond our own homes.

Our principal at the Osterville Elementary school, Miss Sherman, had all the students collect newspapers. We saved our own and asked others who didn't have children in school to save theirs. Our goal was to sell enough newspapers to purchase a film projector for the school.

A truck would come from I know not where, and pick up the papers every week or so. Eventually we were able to buy the projector. All of us felt proud of the fact that we had helped accomplish this.

At home, everything was saved that could be used again. Loaves of bread in those days, came in waxed paper, which my mother reused by wrapping our sandwiches in it. Clothes were recycled in a hundred ways. First they would be handed down to the next one that they would fit.

When they had outlived their wearability, their life was not over. Wools were cut up to make rugs. Cottons would end up as aprons, potholders, dishtowels, etc., etc., etc.

One thing I remember is that my great-grandmother kept a scrap bag full of materials salvaged from clothes. She'd let me pick out several patterns that appealed to me. Then we'd cut them into small squares. After we had them cut and stacked into neat piles, we'd sew them together, alternating patterns to create patchwork pillows. I was very young and a quilt would have been too great an undertaking, but the pillows were a perfect project.

We saved string and boxes of any kind. Oatmeal boxes were used for storage for months before they disintegrated. Plus the dog and cat thought they made great toys.

It was unheard of to purchase new wrapping paper each Christmas. Our wrapping paper was carefully folded after opening a gift. Sometimes we would recognize the paper that had wrapped a certain gift the year before and it would bring back that special moment all over again.

Milk bottles were washed and left on the step each morning and tonic bottles were returned at two cents a piece. Buttons were removed from any unwearable clothing. Every home had a button box.

I'm sure I am forgetting other ways we recycled, although it wasn't called recycling then. Our parents called it "making do."

Saturdays

Saturdays have always been special. They still are. To most people, they are the best day of the week. Sundays are special, also, but they always had a sameness that Saturdays didn't. Sunday was pretty cut and dried, big breakfasts, Sunday School and church, read the Sunday paper, Sunday dinner, then a short time to play before rushing home to listen to The Shadow.

Saturdays could be unpredictable and yet relied on for the certain important things that we counted on.

Of course they were great because after five days of getting up early, dressing in clean dresses and going off to school, it was wonderful to put on some crummy, old beat up slacks and not care that much about appearance.

Saturdays were for rising early because you wanted to and not because you had to. It was knowing your mother was going to do her baking that day and maybe that would be the Saturday she let you make pie crust, or she would make those special tarts you loved so much.

The house I grew up in had three apartments. We lived upstairs, my great-grandmother on one side downstairs. The other side was rented.

During World War II, Mrs. Ashley lived there with her son and daughter. She baked on Saturdays, too, but her specialty was doughnuts.

That woman made the best doughnuts in the whole world... not that I ever had one... They were for the adults.

What her daughter, Mary, and I had were the doughnuts' holes.

We'd wait patiently outside on the kitchen steps while the wonderful smells from the kitchen seeped out to us. When the batch of doughnuts were done, Mrs. Ashley would throw the dough from the doughnut holes into the fat. While they were frying, she'd spoon a small amount of granulated sugar into a brown paper bag. Sugar was rationed during the war so the sugar was an extra treat.

When the doughnut holes were done, she'd drain them on paper for a few minutes, then scoop them into the bag and give them a good shake.

We watched through the kitchen door with mouths watering as she went through this routine. Then she'd come out onto the steps, bag in hand, and give it to us, knowing we would return the bag for refills in about two minutes.

I can picture her standing there, wiping her face with her apron, her round cheeks red from the heat, her hair back in a bun, with wisps hanging loose, touched by flour where she'd brushed them back.

No doughnuts or holes have ever tasted so good since.

Saturdays were not complete without trudging six miles to Hyannis to see the serials which ran only after the Saturday matinee at the Center Theater in Hyannis. All the surrounding villages were deserted by children then.

If we were lucky, we would have earned a little money to buy something to eat from the candy machine, and on a really special day, we might have a sundae at Mitchells across from the theater. That store served the best hot fudge anywhere.

Coming home after the movies was always a good Saturday adventure. We'd act out the heroics we'd just seen, at least until we were too tired from walking.

Sometimes we'd get rides from folks from the village. There were a few whose cars were still on the road and not up on blocks for the duration because of lack of tires or in their yards till they could get more stamps for gas.

When I'd get home from the movies, my great-grandmother would usually send me down to Phoebe Ford's for a half pint of her baked beans. Phoebe ran a boarding house and baked huge pots of beans every Saturday for her boarders and sold them to anyone else in the village who wanted home-baked beans without the fuss of making them.

These were the Saturdays of my childhood and although they have changed some, I still find it a very special day. Don't you?

Shoes Were Made For Walking

Recently I watched a segment on television about a new product called Aqua Shoes. The shoes are for people who like to walk in or at the edge of the water at beaches.

This is a new concept?!

We were wearing rubber beach shoes before World War II. How we hated them! They were made to protect our feet from shell cuts.

One of the main joys of swimming was the freedom from encumbrances; just a suit was fine. When we swam in the ponds or the beaches on the sound, we didn't have to wear the shoes but at the beaches on the inner bays where there were lots of broken shells our parents insisted that we wear them.

Half the fun of walking the edges of the ocean was feeling the sand between your toes and sliding away under your feet. What were a few cuts compared to that?

I shopped the other day for a pair of walking shoes. I picked out three pairs that appealed to me. When the clerk came, he asked what I was going to be using them for. When I told him, walking, he said that none of them were for that. One was an aerobic shoe, one for running and one was a court shoe. I finally settled for a cross-country pair.

I was reminded again how complicated life has become. We are given more choices than we need.

We used to have a pair of everyday shoes, and a pair of Sunday shoes. These were polished weekly, repaired frequently, either by a cobbler or as a do-it-yourself project, like glueing on new soles. Before repairs, cardboard was a temporary solution.

In the summer we received a pair of sneakers which had to last till school started in the fall. The boys wore high tops which we girls coveted unless we were made to wear them. Then it was a different story. By the end of the summer, all sneakers were in shreds. Four or all five toes were through the tops and the rubber strips on the sides were hanging by a thread.

In the winter snow or rainy weather, we wore rubbers or galoshes that had metal fasteners. Ugly! The boys wore high-cuts. If we were really lucky, we might get a pair of rubber boots for Christmas.

Our shoe wardrobe was very limited, but at least we didn't have to waste precious time deciding which shoe was right for which occasion.

We had few choices, and of course the favorite, one which I neglected to mention, is obvious.

Accept for cold weather, our choice was to wear none of the above!

The Old Ball Field

They're disappearing fast. As houses go up, fields are lost forever.

Usually a ball field came into existence unplanned. It became a place to play simply because a family with an extra piece of land beside or down the hill from their house let the children use it as a ball field. Of course, the neighbor's children came to play.

Soon the field became a neighborhood field, adopted totally by all the kids in the area. The only concession to original ownership, was that it was usually named after the family whose land it actually was.

Quite often there were two or three ball fields in a village. Teams would be formed according to which field was the nearest to home, or by ties of friendship. There were no hard and fast rules about who could play. Everyone was welcome and each team had some kids that never could play the game with any skill, but were included anyway, just because.

"Just because" could be any number of reasons, such as, "He's my kid brother. Give him a chance." It could also mean that he had a pretty sister the petitioner wanted to impress with his kindness." "He's only a little kid. Give him a thrill."

Our field was known as Wright's field. A street from the center of the village led to North Bay. A few hundred yards down the road was a steep hill. To the right of the hill was a hollow which became Wright's field.

The Wrights had three boys and a girl. There were six families nearby with as many children or more. The field belonged to us all. We never thought about ownership then. It was just there.

The bases were marked by the fact that there was no grass growing where they were, just dirt from so many kids sliding into the spot. The pitchers mound was the same. Seasons of scuffing

45

around it before winding up had left a dusty or muddy mound, depending on the weather. It was never smooth. Roots and pebbles were mixed with the dirt. Nobody ever complained.

On one side of the field was a huge blackberry patch which we all tried to get to first when the berries ripened. The only bad part was the big black and yellow spiders that guarded them. Plus the briars didn't make the picking berries or retrieving foul balls easy.

On the other side of the field, was the beginning of Mr. Jacob's garden which the boys (and sometimes the girls) considered fair game. His watermelons were never safe from the boys and we girls were known to harvest a few potatoes to eat raw as our dinner while we were playing house in the old lilac bushes nearby.

Much of the fun for the boys was the reaction of Mr. Jacobs. If he saw them near the edge of his garden, he would shout and chase them away, making it a real game for them.

As it became too dark to play ball, we would end the evening playing kick the can, or hide and seek. The younger ones would drop out as they were called home for bedtime. When the game was to be ended, a call would go out for all those still in hiding.

"Allie-allie in free" would bring everyone in and the game was over. Then the older ones would sit around talking until long after dark... maybe waiting to visit Mr. Jacobs garden.

Wright's field has had a big colonial house sitting at the edge for many years now and most of the other fields have been sold as house lots and built on.

Sometimes, though, if you're out walking at dusk near what was an old Ball Field, stop and listen. If your mood is just right you may hear echoes.

"You're out!"

"Am not!"

"By a mile!"

"No way!"

"Allie-allie in free"

46

Tea Parties

The path to Joshua's Pond cut through the woods at the end of Blossom Avenue, off Main Street. A little beyond the other houses, beside the path, was a pretty white cottage. I remember a garden and a fence with roses on it in the summer. Mr. and Mrs. Chase lived there.

Sometimes we stopped to visit with Mrs. Chase. She was a very gracious, elderly lady. At least she seemed elderly to us at the time.

Occasionally she would invite us to an afternoon tea party.

We quite often had tea parties of our own but they were quite different from hers. We had little painted tin tea sets, which we set out with the teapot filled with water and perhaps a little sugar in the sugar bowl. Our imaginations did the rest.

Having tea with Mrs. Chase was like a fairy tale. Our vivid imaginations couldn't have conceived the reality.

We dressed for the occasion.

When we arrived, we saw the table was set with exquisite china. There was a linen table cloth and a real linen napkin for each of us! Mrs. Chase served our tea from a beautiful teapot and offered us delicate cookies, the likes of which we'd never seen. This experience alone was unforgettable but there was more to come.

We waited as patiently as small girls could for the biggest treat of all. After we had drunk our tea and eaten our cookies, Mrs. Chase read the tea leaves that had settled in the bottoms of our cups.

What wonderful dreams she gave us! We would be rich, famous, and travel the world over. We would grow up to be beautiful, marry somebody rich, who would also be handsome, kind, intelligent, and every other superlative she could come up with. In the meantime, all we had to do was not talk to strangers, obey our parents, work hard in school, be kind to everyone and wait for our marvelous futures.

It was an exhilarating experience. It fed our hopes and dreams. It gave us an opportunity to be ladies for a while, to touch and handle beautiful things that our homes didn't have. When our lives seemed dull, dreary, sad or hard, we knew it wouldn't last forever, because we knew what the future would bring... thanks to Mrs. Chase.

what the well dressed young lady of 1939 wore to tea

Tower Hill

What we call the Tower Hill section of the village was mainly woods when I was a child. At the end of Blossom Avenue, was a path through the woods to Tower Hill Road. It came out near the Whiteley and Marney houses. They are on Tower Hill Road between Sams and Joshuas Ponds. The Marney house is known as the Robert West house.

My father used to take us to the Tower Hill section to chop down our Christmas trees. I don't think he asked permission from anybody, but I'm not sure. It seemed like it was just woods and anybody could use it. We children certainly did.

Frankie Adams had a camp near his house on Pond Street and Dick Cross had one near his house on the other side of Tower Hill Road near the old water tower. We belonged to one camp or the other at different times. We fought mock battles, and had spies. We traveled through the swamp that runs from Pond Street to Sams Pond then we went overland a short distance, then back into a swampy area till we reached Tower Hill Road near where the A&P is now. In the winter months we could skate most of the way. I lived where the art gallery and Osterville Radio and T.V. is now and all I had to do was cross the street, go back of what is now Alger and Schillings office and beyond the field was the swamp. Once I was there I could travel on top of the saplings which were laid down to make trails or on ice in the water.

Just about the time World War II began, the Lebels put in some foundations for some houses in the Tower Hill section. I guess the war halted their plans for a while because the foundations were not built on for some time and became marvelous forts for us to play in and around.

The area was full of mayflowers, and blueberries in their seasons. We kept an eye on them and were always on hand when

49

picking time came. We also picked huckleberries when we couldn't find blueberries. They had a delicious flavor but were a little seedy. The worst thing about them, however, was that when you ate them, they stained your mouth blue for a while.

One day a friend (boy) and I picked quite a few, so my mother made us a small pie to share. After supper that night when we all met to play, we two took a lot of teasing with our blue mouths.

The old water tower stood on the hill and overlooked the center of the village. It was often the center of attention. The steps up the side of it were always a challenge for someone. At some point during WWII, it was fenced and guarded by soldiers so that our water supply would not be threatened.

The most exciting thing that ever happened at the tower was when some of the older boys in town (they shall remain nameless) smuggled a dummy that looked very lifelike from a distance, up the tower.

They planted some cohorts up on Main Street, who called attention to the tower, where the culprits were waiting to stage a fight. Everyone watched in fascination and then in horror as the dummy sailed through the air to the ground.

It was the topic of conversation for weeks.

Walking

Most mornings, I try to take a two-mile walk. Sometimes weather interferes. Often it's an early appointment that can't be avoided. I love to walk but just can't always fit it in.

How different it used to be! We walked everywhere. It was most often from necessity. If we wanted to play with someone in Centerville, we walked. We had regular softball games with a team from Marstons Mills. We played at the school which was two miles from the center of our village. We walked over and back. We thought nothing of it. Sometimes we walked over to the Mills to skate on Gifford's little pond which was so small it didn't even have a name. It seemed like a good idea at the time. That's the key word... time. We had plenty of it.

World War II changed our walking habits. We walked more.

Although some of us had bikes, even those became victims of WWII. I got my bike just before the war started. I used it until the tires wore out. Dad patched them for as long as possible and then I couldn't use it anymore because we couldn't buy rubber tires for it. Our family car spent most of the war years up on blocks for the same reason.

It is approximately two miles from the center of Osterville to the lights in Centerville, one mile to Dowses, about a mile to the Oyster Harbors bridge, seven miles to Hyannis. It wasn't as dangerous walking then. The roads were not busy. Between the tire shortage, and gasoline rationing a lot of cars were sidetracked for the duration.

Of course, the population was much smaller then. Incomes were also less. A two-car family was almost unheard of. The car industry boom hadn't begun.

On summer evenings about six o'clock, I would walk down to West Bay Field with my grandfather to watch the softball games. There would be villagers coming from every different direction.

51

Nobody drove a car to the games. Sometimes a boy would race up behind us on his bike and jump off the curb just before reaching us, jumping back on the sidewalk again after passing.

There might be a couple of pickup trucks at the field, that had brought equipment to the game, but mainly everyone came on foot.

It was not a silent march to or from the game. There was good-natured banter between the walkers about who was going to win, or who had won and how and why. It was a friendly time.

Saturday afternoons we were drawn into Hyannis to the theater as if by a magnet.

After lunch, there would be a mass exodus from the village. Small groups of children would start the long trek to Hyannis, because after the matinee there would be a serial, usually Tarzan, or something equally thrilling.

Anybody driving to Hyannis on a Saturday afternoon expected to pick up as many children on the way as could safely fit in the vehicle. Some days we were lucky and some not.

We had a wonderful time, but I certainly couldn't do it now. Just the thought of trudging those seven miles makes me want to go take a nap.

Weapons of Childhood

The weapons of childhood are many. Water seemed to be the ultimate. We splashed each other with it, dunked each other in it, and if we were lucky enough to gain control of a water pistol, the feelings of power were overwhelming but scary. Scary because we knew that eventually somebody would take the gun away. When that happened, we would be made to pay dearly for our moment of glory.

There was one way of using water as a weapon that the boys were adept; puddle stomping, perhaps because of their bigger feet. The idea was to tromp in the puddle in such a way that the water flew sideways at the victim and not upwards over the perpetrator. It was possible to drench the poor victim completely, while the assailant ran away laughing and dry. It was amazing.

Do children still do this?

Some childhood weapons stay the same for countless generations, while others are added and dropped periodically.

Sling shots used to be fairly common, but I haven't noticed them hanging out of any back pockets lately.

Stone and rock throwing are taboo now. There is no longer a "boys will be boys" attitude condoning this practice.

Name calling is probably a close second to water as a weapon. It's one of the most devastating and can have a long acting residual effect.

We yelled "Sticks and stones will break my bones, but names will never hurt me," but they did. We'd cover our ears and yell the foregoing phrase over and over. Pretty soon everyone would be yelling so loudly that no words could be distinguished. Finally both sides would run out of breath and voice.

One weapon that was never used in our youth, was food. As children of the depression, food was scarce. After the depression came World War II. Many foods were rationed. We grew up with a healthy respect for food.

Even to see a food fight on T.V. jars me.

Our kids think they're funny. A son-in-law who was in high school in the late sixties tells about a large stainless steel bowl filled with ripe olives that was at the end of the lunch line. Students could help themselves to them, which they did. But they didn't eat them. They filled their pockets and threw them at each other, in the cafeteria, classrooms and halls. The janitors swept them up from everywhere. The supply of ammunition seemed endless.

Tattling was a two-edged sword. The tattler usually put his victim out of commission for a while but sometimes tattling back-fired. A tattler was never popular.

Girls were more proficient at it and got away with it more than the boys.

A girl could say, "I didn't want to tell but I was afraid some-one would get hurt," or "I didn't know what else to do," or "I thought you'd want to know."

These reasons were all recited in a voice which reflected the tattlers reluctance in telling. If she were a good enough actress she was home free, and could stick her tongue out at her victim and walk away, triumphant for the moment.

The Wig

One summer evening when I was ten years old, my parents were not home and there was a thunderstorm raging. I was trying to go to sleep, when I heard my great grandmother calling.

"Anne," she called in her quavery voice, "There's quite a storm going on. Would you like to come down and we'll keep each other company?"

I smiled, remembering that Grandma was more frightened of storms than I.

"I'll be right down," I called.

54

A few minutes later when I walked into my great grandmother's apartment, there stood a stranger. At least that's how it seemed to me for a moment. A little old lady stood there in her robe and sparse, white hair, caught up in a small top knot. My great grandma had sort of beigy gray hair parted in the middle and drawn back in a bun. This person also had no glasses or teeth. I just stared.

Grandma must have noticed my consternation, because she quickly covered her mouth and said, "I'll be right back, dear."

She disappeared into the other room and then came back with her teeth in.

She motioned me to sit down in the chair opposite her old wicker rocker which she always sat in. She took her glasses from her robe and put them on. They didn't do her much good as she had cataracts, but with each step, she looked more like herself, except for her hair.

She seemed a little embarrassed by my reaction to her.

"I guess I was so upset with the storm, I forgot myself. I don't usually appear to guests in such disorder."

"Oh, Grandma, I'm not a guest," I exclaimed. "It's just you looked kind of different. I've never seen you with your hair like it is, and without your glasses."

I didn't mention the teeth.

"Why, Anne, I've worn a wig for years. My hair became so thin, I couldn't stand it. I guess I'm just a vain old woman."

I couldn't believe that for the last six years we'd lived with Grandma, I'd seen her every day and never noticed.

She leaned back and closed her eyes, rocking gently. Then she spoke.

"I had the most beautiful auburn hair when I was young. As a matter of fact, I still have some. You wait here and I'll show you."

She went into her bedroom and soon came out with a box.

"These are momentos I've kept over the years, ever since I was a girl."

While the storm crashed around us, she took me back through the years. Finally she found a large envelope. She shook it open, and a long auburn braid fell from it.

"There," she said triumphantly. "This is what my hair looked like when I was young."

"Oh, Grandma, how beautiful you must have been!"

My eighty-three year old great grandmother beamed at me.

"I wasn't beautiful by any means, but my hair was. Your great grandpa said it was the prettiest hair, he'd ever seen."

She wandered off into her private thoughts for a minute and then perked up again and took more items from the box telling me about each one.

The evening flew by and neither of us had noticed the storm had ceased.

The next day, when I went in, Grandma looked as usual. Her wig was firmly in place.

Soon after that occasion, her son, my great Uncle Warren, visited her from Providence and brought a gift. It was a lovely silver gray wig.

Grandma seemed pleased and tried it on for us, but after Uncle Warren left, she put it back in its box and put her regular one on.

She patted her apron and hair and said, "That new wig is too fancy for every day. I'll wear it on Sundays." Then she added, "And when they lay me out."

From then on, that's what she did. Six days a week she was the same Grandma I'd always known, but on Sunday it was different. Then she'd put on her Sunday best, including her fancy wig, sit in her rocker holding her best embroidered handkerchief and receive company.

When Great Grandma died at age ninety, she was laid out in her Sunday best and her fancy, silver, gray wig.

It's a funny thing but I can't remember what she looked like in that wig. I just remember her in her everyday one, making floating islands, a delicious custard with meringue, sewing patchwork pillows with me while we listened to her soap operas, and eating pantry cookies and milk while she shared her memories with me.

No wonder I'd never noticed she wore a wig until the night of the storm. We'd just been too busy enjoying each other.

Great-Grandma as I remember her

The Wizard of Oz

It was 1939. I was six years old. The depression was still in full swing. There were rumors of war.

Most of these things went over my head, lost in childhood as I was.

I had been anticipating first grade. I already knew how to read and write. I couldn't wait to start school.

Then it happened.

About two weeks after school started, we were lined up in the hall. A school nurse checked each of us for head lice. I was yanked out of line. Head lice in those days was considered a disgrace. I was quarantined for three weeks.

I had picked them up from a family in the village where I had stopped to play while on my paper route. To add fuel to the fire, my mother had specifically warned me not to go into their house because they were usually unsupervised.

My idyllic childhood came crashing down.

My mother refused to cut my long blond hair as was recommended, and instead shampooed it every day and ran a narrow tined steel comb through my tresses twice daily for weeks. She was none too gentle, because of my disobedience.

Life was becoming a nightmare. My brother was in the sixth grade at the time. Even though he had no signs of infestation, he was quarantined a week. He was furious with me and never lost an opportunity to give my arm a paralyzing punch whenever he was near.

Finally my confinement was over and I returned to school. I was beside myself with happiness. Everything would be wonderful again. How wrong I was! Life had taken a cruel turn. Nicknames were hurled at me, "Bugs" being the favorite.

Former playmates shunned me. Soon my report cards began to reflect the treatment I was receiving at the hands of my fellow students. "Does not work and play well with others," appeared each term on my card. Academically I did fine, but socially I was an outcast.

Fortunately, the movie theater was only a few hundred yards from our home. I went there almost every day, sometimes to watch the shows, sometimes just to visit, or help out.

When the *Wizard of Oz* came, I went to see it and from the moment Dorothy stepped out of her house in Munchkin Land with Toto clutched in her arms, my life changed for the better.

It completely captivated me and has ever since. It was my escape from this world from which I had experienced rejection and hostility and transplanted me to another, where even though there were wicked witches, they received their just desserts in the end... by a young girl and her strange but wonderful friends!

When, two months later, my Dad brought home a small black and white puppy with a curly tail like a pig, naturally I named him Toto. What else?

By then, I had discovered that that first story of Dorothy in Oz was but the beginning. There were several books about Dorothy's adventures in Oz. I read the complete set at least seven times.

I read all kinds of books, but the Oz books were a balm to my soul. I bought the set when I was married and have it still.

When our children were young and the movie came on television, I never missed watching it with them.

Eventually, other obligations interfered and I'd miss it.

About ten or twelve years ago, my husband gave me the video for Christmas. It was one of the nicest gifts I ever received.

Now when there's a gray day, or a blue day, or just a day when I need to get away from it all, I find my out of this world friends and cavort in strange lands.

Then for few days if you pass me, you'll probably see me smiling and hear me humming, "We're off to see the wizard, the wonderful wizard of Oz."

Seasons

May

May always seemed to be the wakeup month after the winter. March is entirely unpredictable and April fluctuates in its moods almost as much as March. We can get temperatures in the eighties as if it were summer, or a snowfall, covering the daffodils, reminding us that winter isn't over yet.

May has its moods, but when I look back, it seems like May was usually generous with its gifts.

On the first of May, we hung May baskets on doors of some of our neighbors. We worked and planned for days, deciding what to put in them and when and how we would hang them without being caught. Half the fun was surprising the recipient.

The day before hanging the baskets, we assembled whatever was going into them. We would have penny candy, usually kinds that were not our favorites so we'd be less tempted to eat them.

Mrs. Wright was the first one on our list for a May basket. She lived up a little lane off Bay Street, but the house could be seen from Main Street. We went to see Mrs. Wright often, because she always welcomed our visits. She was usually working on mounds of ironing, but would stop long enough to give us a treat and then would continue her ironing while we chattered away. We also hung May baskets for our mothers, grandmothers, Mrs. Kalas and a few other neighbors.

On the last day of April, we would go to our secret place to pick mayflowers for the baskets. There was a special spot off Parker Road on a short woods road among the trees on the golf course. The mayflowers were always there early and full. They had large pink blossoms, and a fragrance that was the sweetest in the world. We'd make quite a production of getting in and out of there without being seen.

The next day, May 1, we'd meet before school (unless it fell on a weekend) fill the baskets, which were made from brown paper bags that we had colored. We glued hearts made from construction paper and put extra glue on the handles, of course.

We slipped behind trees, giggling as we went, scooching down if we saw someone through the windows. Then when everything seemed clear, we'd race to the door, ring the bell or knock, then run like the wind for a hiding place that we could see from.

Soon we were rewarded. Someone would come to the door, find the basket and exclaim in a loud voice (for our benefit),

"Someone has left us a May basket. Candy, and mayflowers! Don't they smell wonderful!"

After the door shut, we would creep away until we were sure we couldn't be seen. Then we'd dance around and congratulate each other on our successful trick. What a good time!

At school we would sometimes have a Maypole and wind the crepe paper around it, intertwining it by marching by each other in a special pattern.

After May Day we seem to settle into our spring rituals. Out came the marbles. The school grounds would be filled with small holes used for the games. London Bridges would echo across the yard and the boys would check the thermometer to see if the temperature had reached fifty degrees yet. Miss Sherman the principal wouldn't allow the children to play ball until then. She was afraid they would ruin their arms by throwing hard when it was cold.

By the middle of the month, some hardy souls had been swimming and all of us had been wading, which usually ended with us falling in "accidently."

May produced myrtle, violets, and lots of small wildflowers, including the always prolific dandelion, but the ones that ended up in every child's Memorial Day parade bouquet were lilacs.

Some years they would be just perfect and other years they would be pretty well gone by when we picked them for the march, but there was always enough if we looked hard enough. The light lavender ones were usually plentiful but the deep lavender and the white were harder to find and made a bouquet extra special.

Memorial Day was always on the 30th, but we had our school services on the last school day before the holiday. As soon as the parade and speeches had ended and we had put flowers on the graves, school was dismissed for the day.

By Memorial day, everyone had been swimming, and a wonderful month was ending. For us summer had begun.

* * *

Mayflowers

The mayflower, our state flower, is on the endangered list and cannot be picked lawfully. In our childhood days, mayflowers were abundant.

The snow was barely off the ground when we were scouting out our patches. We had hidden spots in the woods, around the golf courses and along the edge of certain roads.

On our first excursions, we'd pull the dead leaves aside to reveal the green immature leaves huddled there. It was moist under the leaves with a wonderful earthy smell. We'd gently brush the leaves aside to hurry the blooming process.

After checking out each place, we came back weekly to keep an eye on the progress of our patches. We were careful not to let anyone see our coming or going. There were mayflower thieves, you see! All patches were fair game for poachers. While making our weekly surveillance trips, we'd explore the woods for new patches.

Waiting till the mayflowers were ready to pick was hard, but eventually, usually the last of April or early May, they were ready, big, pink and white, and smelling so good, you wanted to eat them.

We'd been taught early that because mayflowers grew vine-like along the ground, we were to hold the vine while breaking off the stem. Otherwise the vine would be torn away and the plant ruined for years.

After picking, we took off the excess leaves, wrapped each bouquet in waxed paper and gave them to our mothers, or sold them.

Over the years, the woods which were hosts to these fragrant flowers have all but disappeared. Careless stripping of the vines has also contributed to the mayflower's demise.

Last spring as I was driving a main road out of the village, I spied some familiar looking leaves on a banking. I pulled to the side of the road to see if they belonged to some mayflowers. They did.

I waited till after a few cars went by, their occupants eyeing me curiously. Then I knelt and poked the leaves away.

There they were! Huge blossoms with that long remembered smell. Risking a fine, I plucked three of them from the vine.

They lasted a week and a half in a miniature vase on my window sill, adding fragrance to my kitchen and sweet memories of long ago springs.

Fourth of July

In the nineteen thirties and forties, Cape Cod was still a group of quiet villages, but not on each Fourth of July.

The day before the fourth was especially quiet. Young people were laying plans and the grownups were preparing food for picnics and planning the family fireworks display.

It was just the calm before the storm.

The quiet was usually broken sometime during the early evening of the third. The rat-a-tat-tat of Salutes and Lady Fingers would break the silence.

That was the signal for my grandmother's Airedale, Frisky, to make his trembling way under my grandparents' bed where he would remain, quivering until July fifth. Even then he would have to be coaxed out with some succulent treat.

The children in the village were up at the crack of dawn on the Fourth.

After a hurried breakfast, we would be given our supply of firecrackers and our stick of punk to light them. The youngest of us would have some Lady Fingers, which were very small firecrackers strung together, and some Salutes, which were about an inch and a half long and exploded singly.

The older children, mainly boys, usually had a formidable arsenal. They had all the smaller firecrackers but several larger ones, too. The one that was the most frightening to us girls was the Cherry Bomb. It was named that because it was red and round like a cherry only much larger. The black fuse looked like a stem. I remember one Cherry Bomb being ignited in a large metal barrel. The sound was deafening.

Usually my friend and I would wander around the village setting off our firecrackers here and there. I think we were both relieved when they were gone.

We couldn't let on that we were scared of firecrackers. The older boys would have hounded us like foxes in a hunt.

We knew enough to avoid the center of the village that day. There would always be some boys perched on the drugstore roof waiting to toss a Cherry Bomb or other equally powerful cracker in back of some poor unsuspecting villager. Eventually they'd pick the wrong person to scare and then they'd be chased off. If they were caught their firecrackers would be confiscated, much to our delight.

Most of the firecrackers were gone before noon with a few held back for evening. Families had picnics and cookouts in the afternoon.

Later we'd wait quietly for the evening to turn dark.

At dusk, the sparklers would appear like fireflies around the village.

Most families had Roman Candles and other colorful fireworks which would light up the village. Our family usually walked to the beach to light our sky rockets and candles and send them up over the water.

What a thrill to watch the lights, hear the reports and see the sparks drift slowly into the bay.

With sleep catching up to us, we trudged home. Another Fourth of July was drawing to a close. Tomorrow morning, Frisky would crawl out from under the bed and life would return to normal.

Ants and Blueberries

One hot August when I was about eight, my mother and I went blueberrying in the woods on the water department land. It was always fun to berry with my mother. She could pick berries faster than anyone I've ever known. We weren't allowed to eat the berries while picking, but anticipating the blueberry dumplings, pies and tarts that would come later kept me honest.

This particular day offered the warm sun, beautiful berries and the gentle hum that pervades the woods on a summer day.

I followed my mother at a safe distance, so that I wouldn't get whacked by a snapping branch armed by her passing. I was poking at puff balls and mushrooms when suddenly my foot sank into a rotten stump. I was in it up to my knee. In an instant, small red ants were swarming up my leg and all over me. I yelled for Mom and she came crashing through the woods like a mother bear rescuing her cub.

I certainly needed rescuing. I had disturbed the biggest anthill I'd ever seen and the ants were mobilizing for war. Mom yanked me out, stripped me down and slapped and brushed hundreds of ants off me, but not before several had gotten their revenge.

A few minutes later when I had calmed down to the level of quiet sobbing, she pointed out how lucky I had been.

Lucky! How could you call what had just happened to me, luck?

My ever practical mother suggested that I could have broken my leg when I fell or even worse, it could have been a wasps nest that I stumbled into instead of ants.

By then, she had soaked her handkerchief in the water she had brought for us to drink and was patting it on my bites.

I stopped crying. I felt a little better about the whole thing, after considering the wasps.

We continued picking. Mom wasn't one to leave things half done. She had a ten quart pail and I a five. When our buckets were full, we went home.

I was bruised and bitten, and berried out, but sitting down later to those light, fluffy, delicious blueberry dumplings it all seemed worthwhile.

Just call me Lucky!

P.S. I still don't eat when I'm picking berries and just in case you ever want to try those dumplings, here's the recipe.

Old-Fashioned Blueberry Dumplings
(except for the Bisquick)

1 quart wild blueberries (frozen will do in a pinch.)

1/2 cup sugar, 1/4 cup water, one dumpling recipe from Bisquick box, vanilla ice cream or whipped cream.

Rinse berries in colander. Put into 3 or 4 quart sauce pan with tight fitting cover. Add sugar and water and stir gently into berries. Cover and simmer for 5 minutes.

While mixture is simmering, make up dumpling recipe. At the end of the 5 minutes, drop dumpling mixture onto simmering berries by heaping tablespoons. Cover tightly. Simmer over very low heat for 25 minutes. Do not uncover at anytime during this period. Remove dumplings, cover with blueberry mixture and serve with vanilla ice cream or whipped cream. Recipe may be doubled easily.

Enjoy!

The Basket Lady

It was a soft summer afternoon in late August. We were just lazying around waiting for something to happen. We were actually starting to look forward to fall.

Then the basket lady came to town and we, grownups and children, had a whole new topic of conversation for days. I'm sure there were different basket ladies over the years but the one I remember was rather plump. She had a full skirt with a petticoat under that you could see a little, and over her blouse she wore a shawl. Baskets adorned her weather wrinkled brown arms like giant bracelets.

As she took the baskets off and spread them out on the grass to show my mother and grandmother, neighbors wandered over and soon there was a fairly large group gathered. There was a tension in the air that had nothing to do with the sale of baskets.

We all knew that this woman was a gypsy! The word gypsy to us had many connotations. They were people you got sold to if you were really bad, and they had second sight. (We children were not quite sure exactly what that meant, but it sounded impressive.) Tension was mixed with anticipation. Although the adults publicly "poo-pooed" fortune telling, they all knew that when you bought a basket, the lady would read your palm, and they all let somebody talk them into it. I jumped up and down and begged my mother to buy something so that I could have my palm read. She did.

The gypsy lady was fascinating and scary at the same time. Her wide-brimmed straw hat didn't hide her piercing black eyes. When she grasped my hand, the thrill that raced through me was laced with fear. She turned my palm up and traced her finger down my lifeline. She never told me anything bad, but sometimes

71

she stopped on a line in my hand and shook her head, saying nothing.

I'd watch her large gold earrings move and try not to look into her eyes. Then suddenly she would chuck me under the chin, smile and tell me all the standard things about travel, love and wealth. Later, I would look at the line at which she had shaken her head, and my spine would tingle. The summer doldrums were forgotten by all of us that afternoon. Fall could wait. We had things to discuss.

Ice

Ah! Summer! It always makes me think of ice. No, not ice cream, ice.

Winter is when most people think of ice, but not me. People who grew up before refrigerators remember ice at its best.

We had iceboxes then, not refrigerators. The ice-man came every few days. Most of the year, we didn't pay much attention to him, but in the summer, he became one of our favorite people.

We waited for the ice man the way the next generation waited for the ice *CREAM* man.

When he pulled into our yard on a hot summer day, the cold icy water would run from the back of the truck as he parked. It would spill onto our dusty feet, turning the dirt to mud as it struck our toes, sending shivers up our backs.

First he'd check the sign in our window to see how much ice my mother wanted. The sign could be turned to display different weights. While he was doing this, we'd help ourselves to small slivers melting in the bed of the truck.

"Out of there, you guys," he'd say, "Maybe I'll give you some when I'm through."

We'd watch as his pick flashed over the huge block, neatly cutting 25, 50, or 100 lbs. pieces. Then he'd take his ice tongs and pick up the newly cut piece of shimmering ice and hang it on the scales, where it would sway and drip while he checked the weight. It was amazing how accurate it was.

After he had collected his money, he'd pull the tarp down over the ice to keep it from melting, then look at us and grin.

"I don't suppose you kids are waiting for a piece?"

We'd laugh at his joke, half afraid he wouldn't give us any. But then he'd throw up the tarp, his ice pick would flash a few times and he'd present each of us with a large sliver of ice that winked and glistened in the sunshine.

Grasping our slippery treasure and thanking him enthusiastically, we'd head for the nearest shady spot to consume that most wonderful treat.

Ice cubes just aren't the same.

Back to School

The children are back in school. Some went with eagerness, some with dread, but most went with new shoes.

Growing up, one thing we could usually count on getting when school started was new shoes. They were not always just what we wanted, but they were new. By summers end, our feet had grown and had spread out from going barefoot, so we had to have them. Sometimes new only meant new to us.

Some of the kids who had brothers and sisters a little older didn't get brand new shoes, but had to wear the leftovers. I was lucky in that respect, because I only had a brother and he was five years older.

During the depression, we were lucky to have anything new.

Dad worked on government projects run by the WPA and was paid in goods such as food and clothing, plus a little money, very little. The result of that was, when school started the WPA gave girls three dresses, which they must have turned out by the thousands in every size. Even though I liked some of the dresses in the beginning, I hated them soon after when I realized that so many of us had the same ones. We were teased unmercifully by those who were not in the same circumstances.

My mother had many talents, but sewing was not one. However, she made the sacrifice and hauled the old treadle machine out of the attic. It took up a lot of space in the center of our small living room, but there it stayed for two weeks while she sewed and groaned at her mistakes. She wasn't particularly happy with the results but I was ecstatic.

I can't recall two of the dresses, but the third was a sailor dress, navy blue with white stars on the sailor collar. I thought was the most beautiful dress in the world. My mother laughed when I said that, and replied that at least it was the only one of its kind. Then she admonished me to be careful not to pull any loose threads because it might all come apart. I knew she was only teasing, but I was careful anyway.

By the time school started, most of us were eager to go. Even the boys who protested against returning, were secretly happy to be back.

The fall lent itself to the outdoor games at recess. Baseball gave way to touch football and Fox and Geese. Marbles were played on the warm sunny days by both boys and girls and London Bridge could be heard on the playground most recesses.

Afternoons when school was out, we would bury each other in leaves, or have rotten apple fights with the "drops" from the many trees around the village.

There were plenty of apples to be had for eating, along with the last of the tomatoes and cucumbers. Watermelons and cantaloupes were still around in the early fall. We managed to pinch a few. Some of the boys made a contest out of it. Sometimes people who had harvested their potatoes would leave the smallest ones which they called "Pig" potatoes. We were allowed to gather them legally.

The squashes were safe from all the kids, but as Halloween grew near, the pumpkin patches certainly need guarding.

That reminds me, I'd better keep an eye on that giant pumpkin on my front steps. I don't think kids have changed that much.

All Falls Are Not the Same

The fall of 1991 would have to come under the heading of strange.

The leaves I am kicking around as I walk the village belong to November, while the lilacs blooming in my yard belong to May.

We have Hurricane Bob to thank for this disruption. Coming in August, as he did, messed everything up. Our hurricanes are usually part of our falls, not midsummers.

We always looked forward to September and October with much affection.

Although it meant going back to school, which the boys protested against more than the girls, it also meant seeing friends who had been away or busy in the summer.

Games in progress when school was dismissed for the summer, were picked up in September without missing a beat. Except for former sixth graders who had moved on, the sides remained the same. Room was made for shy first graders who were included as fascinated onlookers in our games of marbles or Fox and Geese.

Fall meant late season blackberries, picked in Wrights field; watermelons and pumpkins, removed with finesse from Mr. Jacobs garden.

Apples from orchards all over the village were fair game and early fall swims on hot September days were treats never to be forgotten.

As October approached and color rioted everywhere, plans were made for Halloween; parties planned; revenge mapped out for last year's tricks. There was much to do during these benign months before winter.

We managed a little school work, settling into our new classes, learning in spite of ourselves.

Warm days kept us in our summer mode for a while, but as the nights became nippy and the winds brought their chills more often, and we kicked the crisp leaves down the roads, we knew winter was coming.

Kicking crisp leaves now one day and picking lilacs the next is a bit confusing but we'll muddle along and eventually November will come. November can be so depressing, telling us that gorgeous fall days are waning and then ending with the smell of Thanksgiving and the promise of Christmas right around the corner.

Right now, I think I'll go pick a few lilacs and smell summer coming. Perhaps I can fool myself for a few minutes... until I step on those crispy old brown leaves outside my door.

Leaves

As I was out walking early one frosty fall morning, some leaves came skittering down the middle of the road. They snapped and crackled like Rice Krispies. I was busy kicking leaves on the sidewalk, but the sound made me stop and watch the leaves on the road tumble along.

Then I started kicking the sidewalk leaves along again and recalled I've been having a love affair with leaves ever since childhood.

As kids, we played with and enjoyed leaves from spring through fall into early winter, when they disappeared for a few months under the snow.

In the spring we'd pick the heart-shaped lilac leaves and make faces of them by making holes in them for eyes, nose and mouth.

Doing that to a maple leaf gave it an all together different character. It could look like a clown or a king, or like someone who had put their finger in a light socket. Our imaginations soared as we played with these willing pawns.

As spring turned into summer, we used the leaves for cover as we hid in trees to spy out the land around us.

My friend and I had a group of lilac bushes that gave us a house to play in when it was completely in leaf.

77

Making a pile of leaves in the fall was a favorite thing to do. Sometimes we just jumped in them and other times, we hid in the pile and waited to scare someone walking by.

As grownups, of course the fall with its bright array of colorful leaves that has inspired poets and artists for centuries intrigue us, but I think most of us have a special feeling for the leaves of late fall and early winter, when they finally drop off the trees and gradually shrivel up, turn brown and crunchy.

We all say we hate raking leaves, but we do it and the children jump into the piles as children have been doing forever.

We don't burn leaves anymore, but can anyone who has ever forget that wonderful smell, the krinkly sound as the leaves are consumed on a crisp fall afternoon.

I knew we can't burn them anymore, but there's no law that says I can't jump into the pile.

Geronimo!

Thanksgiving

At Thanksgiving, we didn't have to go over the river and through the wood to Grandmother's house.

Grandma, Grandpa and my Uncle Manning lived next door. My great-grandmother lived in the same house that we did.

On Thanksgiving day, we walked across the yard for our feast.

Of course, my brother and I were over there at least ten times before dinner.

Half the fun of Thanksgiving was the wonderful smell of the turkey cooking, not to mention sampling the special goodies placed around the house. There was a bowl of mixed nuts, and another of fruit. In the dish cabinet was a fancy container of after dinner mints waiting to be put out at the appropriate time.

Various pies, fruitbreads, and Grandpa's famous nutcake sat on the sideboard where Grandma thought they would be safe and untouched until after dinner. Long before then, there would be walnuts missing from the top of Grandpa's cake, and the fruitbread slices were spread out a little thinner to make their plates seem as full as when Grandma had placed them there.

In the ice-box were dishes of pickles and olives to be dipped into if no one was watching. Grandpa was more lenient than Grandma about snitching. I think he indulged in it himself, especially the olives.

Grandma came from a wealthy off Cape family and was quite formal with her dinners. Grandpa teased her and said it was because she'd been "born with a silver spoon in her mouth."

One of the best parts of the day for my brother and me (besides the feast itself) was clean up time.

The men always offered to clean up and do the dishes.

The rest of us watched as Grandma almost fainted when my grandfather would wash one of her precious dishes, toss it to my father, who would dry it and sail it to my uncle, who would put it safely away in the cabinet.

After about three dishes, Grandma would be in such a state that the men would be shooed out of her kitchen and the women would take over the chore.

I'm sure this is what the men had in mind all along.

When everything had been put away, my uncle would play the piano and we'd sing a while.

Great-Grandma would sing Thanksgiving hymns to remind us what the day was all about and then we'd go home, knowing that the next day, all those wonderful leftover pies, cakes, turkey, stuffing, gravy, and cranberry sauce would be waiting for us right next door.

More Than Gifts

One of my earliest recollections of the Christmas season in the village was tramping across the golf course, laden with Christmas gifts from my paper route customers.

I was six. I delivered newspapers down Bay Street, ending at the Daniel house, which was the last house on the left before the bay. (It still is.) Then I would cut across the golf course to the intersection of West Bay Road and Parker Road, and deliver papers along there and back to the village center. I had seventeen customers.

It was the first year that I had had a paper route. It was also still depression time and our village was just as poor as most villages in the country. My parents had made it clear that it would be a small Christmas.

That Christmas Eve day as I trudged along my route, I was excited as only a six-year old can be on the day before Christmas. As I stopped at each customer's house, I was presented with a gift. As my paper carrying bag emptied of papers, it was filled with brightly wrapped packages. I had never imagined such a thing. I could hardly contain myself. I also could hardly make it through the snow on the golf course, laden down with all my treasures. It was an unforgettable Christmas.

Christmas caroling was very popular in those days. Some evenings, members of the different churches would go caroling. Other times a group of friends would go. But for the week or so before the holiday, it seemed somebody was always out caroling.

We had a list of people who had a hard time getting out of their homes and some asked for us to sing outside their houses. Some nights were still and brightly lit with stars. Others were cold and blustery. But no matter what the weather we all enjoyed it.

Occasionally, we would be invited into a house for treats. We didn't stay long, because it would be so cold when we resumed our caroling. The thing that always amazed me, and still does, is how wonderful the singing was. I knew all these singers. Some couldn't carry a tune to save their lives, but on those nights we all sounded like choirs of angels.

The caroling at individual houses has sort of faded away through the years, but not the Christmas spirit here in the village. Groups from our churches still carol at nursing homes and other functions. On one special night we all get together uptown to join together in song and wish each other the best of the season.

My Santa

The year I found out the truth about Santa started off like any other Christmas season.

Early on, my mother and I went into the woods and fields around the village to gather evergreens for wreath making. There were several varieties, but the one I remember by name was "Creeping Jenny." It wandered vine-like along the ground.

Mom brought burlap bags to stuff the greens in as we picked. They were the same bags my grandfather used for shellfishing. When we started gathering the evergreens, they smelled of the ocean but by the time we had lugged them home, they smelled of the woods.

My mother's fingers flew as she worked the greens into wreaths. This is how she earned money for Christmas. I tried to help, but known as "fumblefingers" in my family, I wasn't particularly good at it.

In my memory, Christmas was always white and always on a Sunday. Of course, as I grew up, I realized neither was so.

As "The Day" drew nearer, we practiced our parts for the Christmas pageant, went caroling, and nosed around trying to discover Christmas secrets.

The yearly church Christmas party was held in the vestry of the church a few days before the holiday.

My grandfather had been Santa for the occasion for several years, but I had never recognized him.

This time I did.

The minute he came in from the church kitchen with the pack of toys slung over his shoulder I knew who it was.

My grandfather fitted Clement Moore's St. Nick in "Twas The Night Before Christmas" to a T in every way except for the beard. He was round and jolly and his eyes twinkled. His cheeks were rosy. He smoked a pipe and what hair he had was as white as the snow.

My heart swelled with pride as he moved from child to child giving out candy and presents.

When he reached me, he said, "Ho, ho, ho, have you been a good little girl?"

I grinned at him and said, "You know I have."

He laughed and handed me my gift.

I hugged him and said, "Thank you Grandpa."

He looked at me, winked and whispered, "I'm Santa."
I whispered back, "I know you are, but I won't tell."
And I never did.
Until now.

The Lunch Box

Many of my recollections are of traditional Christmas's, while others are of things that happened only once.

This year my memories took me down both paths.

We were cash poor, and perhaps because of it, our parents tried to make Christmas special for us, like the year I asked for ice skates.

My great Uncle Warren used to send a small check each year for gifts for my brother and me. That particular year, my folks had no extra money for Christmas so Uncle Warren's check had to be stretched to the limit.

To make more packages under the tree, my parents wrapped one skate in a gaily decorated box and one in another.

What fun they made of it!

Was there only one skate? Would I have to push along with one booted foot and then glide with the one skate? We laughed and the others opened their gifts, but until I finally opened the box with the other skate, I hadn't really been sure there would be a pair.

I didn't feel poor, I felt lucky.

In our house, mittens and socks were draped on the tree unwrapped, looking bright and new, giving us a preview of our presents.

The hardest part of Christmas for my brother and me was waiting to open our presents.

Some of our Catholic friends opened theirs after midnight mass on Christmas Eve, but most of our friends opened theirs in the morning.

We had our stocking early, but had to wait for the tree until after Christmas dinner was over and everything was cleaned up.

Our parents thought it would make Christmas last longer, but it was agony, watching all our friends in the neighborhood out around with their gifts while we waited to open ours.

One thing that stands out in my memory was my grandpa's new lunch box.

Every Christmas morning, on Grandpa's desk would be a shiny new black lunch box and an orange. That was it.

I thought of my bulging stocking and felt sorry for Grandpa as if he'd gotten a piece of coal.

One Christmas, when I was about six, I told him how bad I felt that the lunch box was all he got for a stocking.

He laughed and said, "Why, that lunch box is the first thing I look for on Christmas. I figure if Santa is going to give me a brand new shiny black lunch box for Christmas, it must mean I'll be around another year. Otherwise he'd just let me use the old one."

During the next year, Grandpa was sick a lot. Finally Christmas time came.

On Christmas morning, I slipped out of the house and sped next door to peek in my grandparents' living room window.

There it was, on Grandpa's desk, black and shiny, his new lunch box.

With a sigh of relief, I raced back home to open my stocking.

Grandpa was safe for another year.

Icicles

The biggest icicle in the world hung from the edge of the roof at my great-grandmother's kitchen door. If there had been a Guiness Book of World Records then, I'm sure it would have been in it.

We don't have icicles like that anymore. I think it's because our houses now are all insulated, where as in those days, they were not. The heat from the stove and fireplaces, went right through the roof, making the snow and ice melt and run down to the edge where it formed giant icicles.

Those icicles could be downright dangerous! We knocked them off from above the doors so we wouldn't get stabbed by them when they fell. We used to eat the small ones and have sword-fights with the bigger ones. These fights only lasted a few seconds. Those icicles were beautifully shaped for swordplay, but not very durable.

When the icicles were melting, it signaled a thaw in the weather, which meant cold, wet feet. When the weather remained cold, our feet stayed dry, cold, but dry. When it was melting outside, our feet were not just cold, but wet and cold.

What a miserable feeling that was!

Socks in those days were usually wool (terrible when wet) or cotton. The cotton ones had no elastic in them to keep them up, so they usually scrunched down and stretched out of shape, ending up in the middle of the wet shoe, where it lumped like an icy stone.

When the feeling became so uncomfortable that we couldn't enjoy what we were doing outside, we'd go in, take off the offending galoshes, shoes and socks, and stick our feet in the oven of the old kitchen stove.

Our feet would be either blue or white when we came in (or perhaps navy or red if the dye in our socks ran) but after warming them a bit, they'd be bright red and itch like crazy.

If something exciting was going on out of doors, we'd just thaw out a little, then put our gear on and head out again. Nothing was dry, but for a while, things were warm and wet instead of cold and wet.

In the evening, some clothes were hung on a rack near the stove, while socks were draped over the oven door. Hats, mittens and gloves filled the shelves at the back, and boots and shoes went under it.

The stove went out sometimes in the night. My mother would light its fire again early in the morning.

When I could put it off no longer, I'd grab what I was going to wear for the day, throw it on the stove to warm and then hop back into bed until I smelled warm wool.

Later, with warm clothes on me and hot oatmeal in me, I'd slip out the door under the threatening icicles hanging from the roof, then dash into a brand new winter day.

Snow

Snow. What a small word for such a complex subject.

We started learning about snow as toddlers and our education concerning it hasn't ended yet.

One thing I am positive of, however, is that no matter what the weathermen tell us there isn't as much of it here now as there used to be.

Of course hindsight always gives us a different perspective, and fifty years of hindsight probably really distorts it.

My first recollection of snow is that it was cold! My second, that it was wet. From there on as I grew, my recollections and observations became more positive.

Snow is one of the most fascinating thing either child or adult will encounter.

All that I learned about it growing up could fill a book. Instead, it filled a good deal of my childhood.

I learned that snow comes in many textures, shapes, depths, any of which can change almost immediately. It grows and shrinks at nature's will. It can be a marvelous plaything or a terrible inconvenience, a danger or a shelter.

Snow is far more than such a small word should allow it to be.

In our kitchen on the second floor of my great-grandmother's house where we lived, there was a small window at one end. Outside the window was a shelf where my mother sometimes put things to cool. What I remember most affectionately about that shelf, was the snow that fell on it. Mother considered that snow clean, as opposed to that which fell to the ground.

The snow on the shelf was snow pudding snow. Special snow to be made into one of winter's delicacies. First my mother would open the window and scoop the white fluffy gift from the heavens into the appropriate number of dessert dishes. She would hand me the dishes which I hurriedly carried to the kitchen table.

As we waited, spoons in hand, she would sprinkle a little sugar over the sparkling snow, then cinnamon. The last to go on, was a small amount of cold evaporated milk. As soon as that hit the dish, she would cry, "Hurry, eat quickly now before it melts!" (as if we needed urging). In less than a wink, there was nothing left in the bottom of those dishes except a little sweet liquid to be wiped up surreptitiously by a small hand.

This same textured snow that snow pudding was made from was also fun to kick into sparkly clouds, or have on the ponds when we skated. It was so light that when our runners whipped through it, it puffed its way to the perimeter of our skating area. There it waited, crouched for that gust of wind which would eventually come and blow it back across the pond to nip at our cheeks before falling to the ice to start the same cycle again.

Other times the snow on the ponds would melt just enough to make bumps. When we tired of tripping over these, we would give up the skating and devote ourselves to using that type of snow for its true purpose. We would make a ball and put it on the ground and start rolling it around. As it moved, it picked up more of its own and we were off. We pushed until the ball was too heavy to move and if help was not forthcoming, we'd stop in our tracks and start another ball. It would be purposely smaller this time in order that we could put it on the first one to make the belly of a snowman.

Usually by this time enough help would arrive and the second part would be completed. The next and last step of making a snowman took a little longer because it required more than snow. Branches had to be found, for the arms. Coal and carrot for the face and something for his head. By the time all arguments about whether he/she should be smiling or mean looking, we had used up enough time and were ready for other important snow entertainment.

As the day wore on and the winter sun beat down, the snow reached the consistency best suited for building igloos or hollowing out drifts stacked up against houses. The boys usually turned to making forts. These were spaced strategically for an anticipated war the following day.

When the forts were finished each team of boys and perhaps a few girls would busy themselves making snowballs for the next day's conflict.

If the weather cooperated and the temperature dropped, the snowballs would turn into lethal weapons by morning. At that point, most of us girls contented ourselves playing in the igloos and drift houses, or stood on the sidelines cheering our favorite team, until such time the boys decided to join forces and take after us with their weaponry.

Gradually over a period of days, the snow would seem to shrink away. We couldn't actually see it melting, but everything we had made became smaller.

Then one morning we'd wake up to the sound of rain on the roof and exit the house to a slushy, cold, wet world, but no matter. Like Frosty The Snowman, we knew that magic ingredient, snow would return again, and we'd stick out our tongue for the first flakes.

Winter

Winter in the village was always a special time. Never mind the chapped lips and faces, or the wet mittens that never seemed to dry completely. We loved the icicles hanging and threatening to get us if we weren't careful, the snow pudding our mothers would make us. We loved everything about the season. We were in our element!

The weathermen tell us that the weather hasn't changed much in the last 50 years, but I find that hard to believe. It seemed that the snow always started around Thanksgiving and lasted through until at least March. In January and February, it miraculously disappeared on the ponds which were then perfectly clear for skating. The nights we skated, there were always small fires around the edge of the pond, where we warmed our hands, or cooked a hotdog. Roasted potatoes were also a big treat, and nothing could beat the taste of a drink of water from the hole in the ice, made for just that purpose. You had to lay flat on your belly to drink and it was the coldest water in the world. The hill on the golf course at the top of West Bay Road was the favorite sledding spot for many. We called it Craigs Hill but in recent years I have heard it called other names. It's still a popular place. One side of the hill was steeper than the other so that you went faster, but the other side was sloped better for distance. At the top of the hill was a small shelter with seats on four sides. It was a unique design. There was always shelter from the wind if you sat on the right side. It was built for the golfers, but I'll bet more children, their parents and young lovers sat on it over the years than any golfers.

Another spot that the kids around our neighborhood had to slide on, was what we called Jesse Murray's Hill. It's official name is Fire Station Road. Mr. Murray was a general contractor and also owned the school bus for our village. When the hill was perfect for sliding, he would not sand the road so that our sliding would stay good. He had a hard time getting his trucks and bus up that hill sometimes but did his best to avoid using any sand. On a perfect run, we could make the whole length of the road.

Sometimes it go so cold that North Bay would freeze over. My mother used to tell me of her family going to visit friends in Cotuit by taking a wagon across the bay. We loved to go down to the shore at the end of Bay Street and play what we called "Bendigo." The salt water was never firm at the shore and as we walked or ran over it. it would bend and the water underneath would move the ice up and down. I'm sure we were not supposed to play on it. It was exciting and dangerous and something we all tried at least once or twice.

As winter drew to a close, there would come a sunny day when the snow was almost gone, with just a few patches left in the woods and meadows. Then we would take a jar of milk and a peanut-butter sandwich, go find a not too wet patch of pine needles and have our first picnic of the year and talk about spring when we would go mayflowering, play marbles, hopscotch, and baseball. We could hardly wait!

Winter's Ups and Downs

When milk came in glass bottles and was not homogenized, winter brought an extra treat. Cream always rose to the top of the bottle. Mother would pour off most of it for coffee cream. It was strictly for the grownups. We were not allowed to touch it.

In the winter when the milkman left the milk on the step early in the morning, it would freeze before it was retrieved. It expanded as it froze, forcing the cardboard cap and the cream upwards. It would extend two or three inches above the bottle.

Sometimes, we children would cut off a slice or two, replace the cardboard cap and enjoy our contraband with nobody the wiser.

In that same era, before homogenized milk, loaves of bread were sold wrapped in waxed paper. Commercial waxed paper was available, but in our family, it was considered a luxury. In winter, we hoarded whatever waxed paper we could get. Our sandwiches were often wrapped in it. After we'd eaten our lunch, we'd fold the paper up to be used later to wax the runners of our sleds and skates. It also helped shoes slide into boots that were often too small.

Winter also brought skating weather. It seemed as if as many grownups skated the ponds as did children. At night it was a family sport. There were usually a few small fires around the pond's edge. We clustered around them to warm cold hands and feet. Sometimes we brought hot dogs or potatoes to roast.

Winter could also have a downside, I discovered one night on my paper route.

I only had seventeen customers in the winter, but I could stretch delivery time into several hours by stopping to play or having a hot drink at a customer's house.

One winter night, as I left my last customer on Bay Street, which borders the golf course, I decided to take a shortcut across the course to finish my deliveries on the other road.

The moon was full and at first, it seemed a cheerful place. The snow had a thick crust on it. I was able to walk on top of the drifts with no problems.

About half way across, a drift gave way under me and I sank to my chest.

What seemed like tons of snow fell in on me, filling my boots, pockets and the cloth bag full of papers that I had slung over me.

At first it seemed funny, but not for long. I was beginning to get very cold. The moon which had seemed so bright and friendly when I started, now cast scary shadows across the snow.

I struggled for what seemed like forever, inching my way out to a spot where the snow had been blown away by the wind and was only a few inches deep. I was free, but half frozen.

I delivered my wet papers and trudged home, resolving after this to take no more shortcuts and to be home before dark.

World War II

World War II

In 1942, our government was mobilizing the armed forces, training men, building planes and doing everything militarily possible to win one of the toughest fights this country had ever been in, World War II.

Hundreds of books have been written about it and documentaries filmed by the dozens.

Everyone knows what went on over there, but what about the happenings here at home? There was the Fat Parade, the airplane spotting program and the search for the elusive milkweed.

A lot of interesting things happened on the home front during the war. We children growing up in our small village of Osterville, on Cape Cod, helped win the war in our own way. One phrase that became familiar to us early in the war was "helping the war effort."

The day after Pearl Harbor, our elementary school principal, Lida Sherman, gave us a long talk. We all felt the shock and thrill of being at war, although we had no real conception of what it really meant. Miss Sherman tried to impress upon us how things would change in our lives. She said that we must be brave and patriotic and as a school we must work together to help any way we could.

We began.

One of the first things we had to do was learn to prepare for an air raid. We were taught how to sit, covering our heads and how to lie on the floor next to the wall in the halls.

Planes flying over our village had been exciting and rare before the war. We'd rush out of our house or stop whatever we were doing to see them. Now the drone of an airplane struck fear in our hearts. We still looked, but only to be sure they were ours.

Soon after the war started, a small spotter's tower was built on the roof of the community center. Stairs led up the side of the building to the spotters tower room. This room had a window on each wall. There was a big chart on one wall, showing all types of aircraft, the Germans' and ours.

We helped cover the shifts in the tower, each young person with an adult. We learned how to recognize all the planes and logged each one that we saw. We took this responsibility very seriously. All those who helped were given certificates for time served in the tower.

The Fat Parade was another way we helped. Once a week, after attendance was taken, everyone in our school lined up outside with our containers of fat. Miss Sherman would walk up and down the long line.

"All right, children, straighten up, shoulders back, good posture. No giggling, girls! Boys, remember, this is for the war effort, so let's be serious."

Miss Sherman clapped her hands sharply and we all quieted down.

It was spring, 1943. We were taking our weekly march uptown to the First National store. All of us had containers filled with leftover grease that our mothers had collected during the week. It was used to make munitions. We understood how important it was to the war effort, so we marched proudly, if somewhat straggly. At the store, each container was weighed, emptied, and given back to us to refill.

We loved the Fat Parade. We got out of school for an hour or so; we were made to feel we were doing something important, and most of all we were helping to win the war. The money our school got for the grease, was used to send subscriptions for the Readers Digest to servicemen from our village.

During those war years, we took part in some activities that would certainly seem pretty strange now. One was gathering milkweed. Before World War II, we were always cautioned not to open the pods of the milkweed, which we loved to do. We'd toss the silky innards to the sky to watch them float away. Of course, we were helping to seed more milkweed, which most adults considered a nuisance plant.

However the war changed all that. Milkweed became a coveted asset. The silk in the pods was used in life jackets. Teachers took their classes on field trips to various parts of the village to stalk the now elusive milkweed. It was another time we were out of school having fun. No wonder we were caught up in a patriotic fever.

One Saturday morning everyone in the village who wanted to help, gathered at the school. We were handed a sack for collecting, and the great milkweed hunt was on. Children and adults drifted to every part of the village.

I remember standing on a high point at the edge of the golf course watching everyone spread out, filling bags, calling to each other when they found a good patch. It was quite a sight.

From that same spot, I could see Camp Have Done It at the edge of West Bay. It was an amphibian base. The young men who trained there, were called Commandos. They were the first ones to hit the beaches with men and supplies in an invasion.

My neighbor, an eccentric, but very patriotic, old lady, named Mrs. Breck would collect anything she could for those soldiers. She often took me with her from door to door, collecting magazines, coat hangers, and writing materials.

Then we'd go down to the camp and deliver them. She would also mail letters and do errands for those who couldn't leave camp. Meanwhile, I would wander around.

While we were there one day, some soldiers were practicing with their drums. They promptly adopted me as their mascot and slung a drum over my shoulder and proceeded to teach me two or three beats they used when they marched. I have never forgotten them — the beats or the soldiers. They shipped out soon after.

Another thing we collected and turned in was scrap metal. It went into a big pile in the center of the village, to be collected and sent away to be recycled into war material. Everything was scarce. When we bought a tube of toothpaste, we had to return the old tube, because the lead in it was needed. The war was intensifying.

Osterville Children 'All Out' for War Effort

Sacks of milkweed were collected for the war effort. This picture was in the Cape Cod Standard Times after a big milkweed hunt.

World War II - Part Two

We were children of the depression, so we were used to doing without because there had been little money. During the war there was more money, but less to buy.

Everybody had a ration book filled with stamps for the things you could buy. Sugar was rationed, but Karo was not, so my mother learned to bake with Karo. Our pancake syrup was made with Karo and a little maple flavoring. Meat was rationed except for organ meats, so we learned to eat kidney stew (I loved it), liver (I hated it!) and bake stuffed beef heart, which was okay.

Gasoline was also rationed, and rubber was practically nonexistent.

Our family was finally able to buy a car, but between no gas and worn out tires, it spent the war years up on blocks where we could look at it, but that was all.

Dad nursed my bike along until the tires were more patches than original rubber, but finally they gave up the ghost. We couldn't even buy patches.

At night we had blackouts. There could be no lights showing. Every house had to have room darkening shades or some other way of blocking out all light. If any escaped, there would be a knock on the door. An air raid warden would tell the occupant to cover the offending beam.

The top half of all headlights were covered with black tape and no street lights or outside commercial signs could be lit. It was dark!

My girlfriend and I lived about a mile apart. When it was time for one of us to go home after dark, we would walk down the middle of the road to the midway point between our homes. Then we'd say goodnight and turn toward our houses, calling to each other every few seconds. When we were finally far enough apart that our call wasn't answered, we'd run as fast as we could through the darkness to the safety of home.

The water tower stood high above the village. There was a ladder up the side of it. Throughout our childhood, someone was always climbing it on a dare, or throwing dummies off it as a practical joke.

When the war started, a large chain fence was put up to encircle it, with guards on duty twenty-four hours a day to protect our water supply.

These precautions gave us material for our saboteur fantasies, which we had quite frequently.

One day we found some beautiful new 78 rpm records under a step at an abandoned house. They were in a foreign language so we called the police. They turned out to be German and Italian operas. We had some great spy fantasies with those. Some poor villager probably thought it wouldn't be considered very patriotic to have them around at that time.

As men left for the service, women and boys took over their jobs. We girls then got a chance to break out of the mold and do jobs that before were exclusively a man's domain.

We were hired for lawn-mowing, weeding, delivering groceries and even caddying. My friend and I only tried caddying once. We had to carry doubles for eighteen holes and even a five dollar tip wasn't enough to entice us back.

Cigarettes were extremely hard to get. The delivery trucks would come into the village about every two weeks. Each store would allow two packs to a family. My parents would send my brother and me uptown to get what we could. There were the strangest brands. The only one I can remember is Oasis. When my dad ran out of cigarettes, he had a little machine that he used to roll his own, using cigarette papers and Bugler tobacco.

Nobody could buy silk stockings. All the silk was being used in parachutes and other war items. The women in our village wore their silk stockings, runs and all for a long time. Then they turned to leg makeup.

I can picture my mother getting ready to go out with Dad on a Saturday night. First she would cover her legs with a tan liquid and let it dry. Then came the amazing part. She would take her eyebrow pencil and somehow draw a straight light up the back of her legs to represent the seams. They were always perfect. Everyone learned to make do.

Later in the war, sometimes when I'd go with my neighbor to deliver things to our men at Camp Edwards, in Bourne. We'd see German prisoners milling around behind barbed wire fences. I didn't want to look at them because they frightened me. I was sure they would get out. I could feel their restlessness. It was obvious even to a child.

After the 1944 hurricane, the German prisoners were in our village on work details most days, helping with the hurricane cleanup. Most of them were very young, and looked more frightened than threatening. One young blond boy with the PW stamped on the back of his shirt couldn't have been more than sixteen. He was working around the pond. My friend and I would smile at him as we walked by. Sometimes he would smile but usually he just kept his head down.

One thing about having the prisoners working in the village was that we came to realize that they were not the terrible Nazis that we usually saw portrayed in the movies, but we were still glad they were under guard.

When the war ended with Germany, we rang the bells in the churches and when Japan finally surrendered, I went to the church to help my grandfather ring the bells again. The sirens wailed, horns tooted and people came into the church to give thanks. Some people started singing *God Bless America*.

Soon after the war ended, a temporary monument was erected in the middle of the village between the First National and the bank. We had a ceremony one Sunday afternoon. Speeches were made, and the Gettysburg Address given. Later a permanent monument was fashioned.

One day recently I went to it to read and count the names. One hundred fifty-three had served in the armed forces from our village. Five of the names had stars beside them, which meant only one hundred forty-eight returned.

I thought back to those war days. We were only children, but we had tried to do our part to help the war effort.

Our water tower was guarded around the clock during WWII.

Our beautiful car with the rumble seat in 1940. It spent the war years up on blocks — no tires — no gas!

Our community center sprouted
a "spotters" tower during WWII.

Places of the Heart

Our Beach

Bay Street was around the corner from our house. At the end of the half mile stretch was North Bay and our beach. It was here that I spent much of my early childhood.

The shore at the end of the street was littered with shells, tossed there by tides and gulls.

We'd walk to the right a ways, then cross a plank my father had laid over the ditch. The plank sometimes was covered with water on a moon tide. Beyond the ditch about a hundred yards was our beach. I thought we owned it, but as I found out in due course, we were just using it. Land and beaches were plentiful at that time and owners didn't mind.

After crossing the ditch we'd slog along in our old sneakers or beach shoes. I hated wearing the shoes, but if we walked barefoot along the shore, the shells would cut us and the eel grass was no kinder. A paper cut seemed nothing compared to shell and grass cuts.

Our parents never worried about wounds received at the beach. Salt water was the cure all. It also stung like crazy in a cut.

"Has to hurt to heal," my grandfather would say. He didn't believe it and neither did I, but he said it anyway, and I'd nod in agreement, and then we'd smile at each other. We figured we'd done our part in the grandfather-granddaughter scheme of things.

To me, the small sandy spot that we called "our beach" was perfect. The eel grass had receded enough to give us a wide sandy path to the water and the shells were sparse in this area. We picked up most others that came our way by air or sea.

Dad and my brother had lugged a fifty gallon drum to the site and without its top, it served as a rubbish barrel. A dune hugged the back of our sandy patch. It kept the wind from us unless there was an onshore breeze.

107

During the week, my mother, brother and I went there most good days. Grandpa was usually somewhere out on the bay, his skiff tied up to the raft from which he was quahogging.

One day during the summer that I was four I unexpectedly learned to swim. Grandpa rowed his skiff to the beach and my mother and I climbed in. We rowed away from shore.

When Grandpa figured we were far enough to be well over my head, he pulled the oars in and told me I was going to swim to shore. Before I had time to protest, he'd tossed me overboard.

I came up sputtering and slapping the water, but was soon paddling like my mother had tried to teach me. Somehow, being out there over my head, made the lessons all sink in and after a few seconds, I got the hang of it. With my mother cheering me on, I struck out for shore.

Grandpa kept close with the skiff and Mom was poised to rescue me if I faltered.

I dog-paddled the distance. My brother stood grinning on the shore.

I was free! No more would I have to be watched like a baby.

The days flew by once I could swim. In no time, I was locating little necks with my toes and going underwater to retrieve them.

I was in and under the water so much that I felt part of it. I used to wish I could breathe under there like the fish so I tried it. It didn't work. My heart belonged to the sea but my lungs wouldn't cooperate.

One Sunday, we were having a picnic lunch, when a giant sea turtle walked out of the water. We couldn't believe it! He seemed bigger than me.

My dad and brother decided to capture him and sell him to Mr. Lovell, a man in town who hunted and sold turtles.

First they turned the rubbish barrel on its side, then they caught the turtle with the blanket and forced him into the barrel. It took all their might to right the barrel with him in it.

We picked everything up and hurried to the village to tell Mr. Lovell about our find.

When my brother told me that the turtle would be killed to make soup, I cried and carried on, remembering the sounds of his struggling in the barrel when we left the shore.

Mr. Lovell went to collect the turtle and miracle of miracles, he was gone. He'd chewed through the metal barrel and had gone back to the sea.

Later our family went back to the beach. Everyone marveled over the jagged hole in the side of the barrel.

Happy, now that I knew for sure that he'd escaped, I decided to go for a swim.

"You're not going in there now, are you?" said my brother. "He's probably pretty mad. He could bite your toes right off."

"Why should he?" I asked, "I'm not the one who captured him. It's you that better hope he doesn't carry a grudge."

And I turned and followed turtle tracks into the water.

Our beach with my brother Earle and our dog Toto. The small black line on the bay is Grandpa quahogging. I must have been underwater.

Bundling – February 1875

Annie yelled. "Ow, Sarah. You're so rough!"

Annie gave her older sister, a dirty look.

"Just because you're five years older and married, you don't have to treat me like a child."

Sarah stopped her brushing and hugged Annie.

"I'm sorry, Annie, I didn't mean to hurt and I don't think you're a child. I know how important tonight is for you."

"Do you, Sarah? Do you really? I know Frank is going to propose to me. I'm sure he's already spoken to Pa." She rushed on. "Pa likes him. He is eight years older than me but I don't care. The other boys seem like babies."

Sarah laughed, "I think Frank has just been waiting for you to grow up, Annie. He's never shown an interest in anyone else that I know of. Now that you're fifteen, I guess he feels it's time he declared himself."

"I wish Pa wouldn't make me wear braids tonight, maybe let me wear it loose, or at least put it in one braid."

"Annie!" said her sister in a shocked voice, "You know you'll be bundling tonight if you and Frank don't want to be right in the midst of everyone. How would it look for you to lie on the bed with one braid as if you were retiring for the night, or worse still with your hair spread out like a bride?"

Annie pouted a little but then looked at Sarah and giggled.

"Pa would have a fit wouldn't he, Sarah?"

Sarah smiled, and said to Annie, "I remember when Herbert and I were courting. Pa made the bundling board himself and inserted the small rectangular squares of glass in the bedroom doors so that he could check on us. I heard him say to Mother that

110

nobody was going to slip over the board in Nathan West's house."

Annie and Sarah covered their mouths and blushed as they both realized what slipping over the board usually meant; an earlier marriage than originally planned.

Later that evening when the family was gathered in the living room around the fire, Annie could feel the cold pervading the edges of the room. She herself was on pins and needles waiting for Frank to arrive. She was aware that Pa had loaded the kitchen stove and set it really low. Banking the fire his way assured glowing embers in the morning for Mother to quickly get a good breakfast fire going.

It seemed late. Perhaps Frank wasn't coming. Annie no sooner thought this and he was at the door. Shortly after Frank came, Annie caught her father's eye. Nathan West stood up.

"If you young people would like to visit alone for a while, mother will bundle you up for a spell."

Annie and Frank followed Annie's mother into the bedroom off the kitchen. The oak bundling board was about six feet long and eighteen inches high. It had a semi-circle cut out of it at the top end, so that the bundlers could see each other and talk. Annie watched Frank help her mother put the board lengthwise down the middle of the bed. Then he carefully took off his jacket and laid it on a chair, before lying down on one side of the board.

Annie watched all this with a pounding heart. She was thinking how much she wanted to marry Frank, when her mother broke into her thoughts.

"Well, Annie, are you going to stand there forever? I'd like to get you covered and get back to the fire."

Annie quickly lay down on the opposite side of the board from Frank. Her mother piled a number of quilts over them. Nothing showed but their heads.

The lamp on the nightstand flickered as Annie's mother went out and shut the door.

Annie looked at Frank, admiring his soft brown mustache and blue eyes. She couldn't think of a thing to say.

Frank broke the silence at last.

"You know, Annie, I'd almost risk your father's wrath and slip over this board to hold you and stroke that beautiful auburn hair, but your wiley mother has piled so many quilts over us, that I couldn't move an inch if I wanted to. I guess I'll just have to wait until we're married."

Annie West found her voice.

"If that's a proposal, Frank Hodges, then I accept."

1944

When my great grandmother told me this story, she smiled and said, "From the time we married till the day he died almost forty years later, there was never again room for a board between us."

The Bay

It calls to me most mornings. Sometimes it sends a messenger over the house. I hear the raucous call of the gull, reminding me that I must go.

I walk down the shaded road and stop at the curve. The bay is waiting in the sunshine, rippling a greeting to me.

I stand, lost in its beauty. Others have come to pay their respects. The gulls announce them all. Two Blue Heron stalk the shore, their shadows preceding them like monster cranes.

A loon is gliding along the sunbeamed waves, lazying between boats that undulate gently at the end of their tethers. The anchors which hold the lines captive, churn the bottom, scattering silt and small life forms.

The light breeze seems to push a pair of Canada geese slowly across the surface.

Another day when I arrive, the bay shows me a glassy image. Everything seems to move in slow motion. Mirrored twins of ducks and geese trail long v's behind them, as they paddle almost in neutral.

It seems so peaceful and yet I feel an undercurrent. The bay's energies are trapped just below the surface and it waits for a freshening breeze to release them. Boats loll. Coromants pose on their transoms ready for flight. Even the gulls are stilled. Waiting. The wind rises. Clouds form and skitter across the darkening sky. The gulls cry out a warning.

The waves seem confused, bumping into each other, spoiling the natural flow. As the rain comes sheeting towards me, I leave hurriedly.

Today when I reach the shore, there is no welcome. The bay has shrouded itself in fog. I hear murmurings. The lines of the sailboats' masts speak softly to each other, but not to me.

The bay has shut out my world and speaks only to its own.

Joshua's in the Moonlight

It was February 1871.

Eleven year old Annie West heard the clock strike midnight. She sat up quickly, slung her long legs over the side of the bed and pulled on her warm woolen stockings. Then she reached for the bundle she'd hidden under the bed.

Her sister Sarah stirred.

Annie froze.

Sarah sighed, mumbling something in her sleep and turned over.

Annie quietly unrolled the bundle which was a pair of her brother Charlie's trousers and slipped them on. Then she tucked her nightgown into them and put on her warm sweater. Next Charlie's barn shoes went on. For once she was glad she had big feet. Finally she tucked her long auburn braid into one of her brother's caps.

She pushed her pillow long ways under the blanket in case Sarah might wake and glance over, then she tiptoed out of the room and down the stairs. As she went past her parents' room she was reassured by her mother's snores. Pa was away on a trip.

Charlie was waiting for her with the skates in the back hall. He put his fingers to his lips and beckoned her to follow him. They slipped silently across the fields until they came to the small scrub pine woods that overlooked the pond.

The full moon had followed them, casting shadows that at another time would probably have sent Annie scurrying for home, but this night was special. Charlie was with her and her heart's desire awaited.

Once they were inside the small woods, Charlie turned and put his hands on Annie's shoulders. Although he was younger, he was as tall as Annie.

"Annie, I know this is really important to you but if Pa finds out, it will go especially hard with you, being a girl and all, even if you are his favorite."

"Oh, Charlie, I'm not his favorite, it's just I'm his youngest daughter. Besides even if I get strapped, it will be worth it."

"Let's hurry!" She dragged at his arm.

They slipped and slid down the bank.

There it was; Joshua's Pond in all its moonlit glory.

Annie's breath caught in her throat. She had skated this pond practically since she could walk, but always encumbered by long dresses, petticoats, and Mama.

She wanted to fly across it like the wind.

Now she was to have her chance, thanks to Charlie. She had confided her dream to him and he had hatched this plan.

Annie put on the skates and looked across the pond. The moon sketched a track for her. She stepped onto the ice and started off slowly. She felt so light. Gradually she picked up speed. She flew down the moon's path, her shadow outskating her.

Finally she veered off the moon's track into the darkness at the edge. She stopped to catch her breath and watch Charlie. She hugged herself in ecstasy. It was everything she'd dreamed it would be. She'd known she could skate as well as any boy in the village.

As her breath slowed and her heartbeat quieted, the dark and cold crept in on her and Charlie seemed far away on the other side of the pond.

For a few seconds, the thrill of the adventure receded, but when she stepped out into the moonlight again, the magic came back with the same intensity as before and she was off again.

115

She whirled, twirled, and dashed every which way. She felt like a dancer, a fairy, a racer, but the most overwhelming feeling was that of being free.

It seemed only a few minutes had passed, when Charlie skated up to her and caught her hand.

"Time to go, Annie. We've been here a couple of hours at least."

"Has it really been that long, Charlie?" Annie said, but even as she spoke she knew it had been.

She held her brother's hand as they skated to shore.

Before she let go, she squeezed it.

They took off their skates, climbed the bank and crossed the fields in silence.

When they reached the safety of the back hall, Annie turned to her brother.

"Thank you, Charlie. It was wonderful! Maybe we can do it again, but even if we do, I'll never forget tonight."

And she never did.

It was 1941 when my great-grandmother, Annie, told me about that night. It had been seventy years before and she recalled it as if it had been the night before.

I looked up at her when she finished the telling. She was rocking back and forth in her wicker chair, with her eyes closed and a smile on her face.

My presence had been forgotten. She was eleven years old again, and streaking across a moonlit pond.

The Sidewalk

It ambles from the main street to the bay. Its beginnings are high in the village where it starts off formally with asphalt and white curbing. As it passes the last store, it relaxes its pose. Having lost both curb and asphalt, it becomes as a cow path from by-gone days. As it turns the corner on its trek to the water, a huge black walnut stands guard over it, dropping, in its season, green nut casings on the unwary.

Grass grows where asphalt was. Dirt pencils a line down the middle, diagraming the way. Large roots weave their way through it. The tall maples being held and fed by the giant roots, line the road and their leaves and branches form a canopy over street and sidewalk. Smaller roots, snaking their way across patches of sidewalk remind of us bygone days when barefooted we'd stub our toes on such as these. Does anyone ever forget that feeling? We'd hold the scraped and bruised toe for only a second or two, before shaking the pain away. It would be looked over and given more sympathy later when the day was done.

The sidewalk moves us along, with one huge maple and its attending roots almost stopping us in our tracks. Its girth has usurped most of the walk between the street on one side and the stone wall on the other. But wait, there is just enough room to sidle around the tree which asks for a touch of our hand. Of course it would be easier to just step into the street at that juncture, but there's a feeling about slipping by that old maple that shouldn't be missed.

Large houses line this same street, but do not detract from the walk. In some places, owners have tried to encourage their pristine lawns to march to the street in front of their homes, but the sidewalk has won out over their efforts. In some spots, grass cov-

117

ers the sidewalk but is matted in the center and will soon become a small line of dirt to guide walkers.

In front of the old lodge and restaurant, the sidewalk turns into concrete, scored by lines, as the large sidewalks in front of the stores uptown were in childhood days. How many times did we chant, "Step on a crack, break your mothers back," as we avoided those cracks whether walking, running, or roller skating.

As we reach the end of the cement sidewalk and grass again takes over, the bay opens up in front of us.

The sidewalk ends abruptly, as if it knows it has lost our attention.

The Shanty

It sits now on the shore looking like a box. It's been reconstructed as a summer place.

It used to be Johnny Crosby's Oyster Shanty.

A small gray weathered building, it perched on the shore of the channel that separated North and West Bay, southwest of the bridge that joins Osterville village to Little Island and Oyster Harbors.

It was a little over a mile by road from our house in the village center. My grandfather walked to it each day to work as a shellfisherman for Mr. Crosby. I rarely took the road when I went there to walk home with Grandpa. Usually I'd shortcut across the golf course, by the boat yards and over the bridge.

Sometimes on my way I'd see Grandpa out on the raft in the bay working his bullrake. I could picture the long double rake.

Each side had sort of a wire half basket attached in back of the teeth to trap the quahogs when the rakes were closed, then it was brought up to the raft to be emptied. Grandpa would take out the quahogs, then brush the rest of the debris off the raft and sink the rake again. He'd let me try it once but all I brought up was seaweed and old shells. It was hard work.

If he wasn't too far away, Grandpa might spy me and wave. I'd wave back and although I couldn't see his face clearly, I'd know he was smiling because I was coming to walk home with him. Then I'd take my time and scour the shore for treasures as I went .

On warm days the doors to the shanty would be open. When I stepped in, spots of sunlight flicked across the walls as the men's knives flew back and forth, shucking the shellfish for the orders that had come in.

The men stood at the long benches with their hip boots turned down, laughing and talking as they worked.

They'd acknowledge me with a smile and nod as I climbed up on a stool to watch them and wait for Grandpa.

Mr. Crosby would tease me about one thing or another, ask about everyone in the family, and still keep an eye on everything going on, his hands working constantly.

If the men were shucking the big quahogs called bulls for chowders, they would usually slice off pieces of the muscle that held the shells together to give to me for a treat, knowing it was my favorite part of the quahog.

Usually I would sit quietly and breath in the wonderful smells that still make me homesick for that place and time. The breeze slipping in the open doors and windows brought the life of the ocean. I could almost taste the salt and the mud and the seaweed that clung to the rocks moving rhythmically with the motion of the tides.

The clams and quahogs had that special freshness that could not be duplicated away from that spot. The oysters and scallops in their seasons had a different smell, softer somehow.

119

Outside the shanty, the empty drying shells that piled up higher than I stood had a chalkiness that powdered my skin and clothes when I handled them looking for special beauties to take home.

Some days my mother, brother and I would take one of Mr. Crosby's skiffs and row over to Seapuit river to spend the day quahogging for him, only we didn't use a bullrake. The river flowed between Dead Neck and Oyster Harbors.

Mom worked near the shore getting the smaller quahogs, little necks and cherrystones, while my brother and I dove in the deeper part of the river for bulls. At the end of the day we would row back to the shanty and sell them to Mr. Crosby. I think we got five dollars for a bushel. That was a lot of money during those depression times and helped support us.

Sometimes when I knew a storm was coming, I'd go to the shanty early, figuring Grandpa would be in earlier than usual if it started getting rough out on the water.

When I'd get there, Mr. Crosby would collar me to help him prepare for what was coming. He had the greatest respect for the storms and hurricanes that frequent our shores. He'd announce that a "big blow was coming" and set me to work helping him get ready for it.

When a storm was coming, he didn't batten down. Just the opposite. He would secure some things, remove others, and then open every door and window. Once I asked him why he did this instead of shutting everything up like most everyone who had shanties did.

"Well, little girl, I figure that instead of resisting Mother Nature, I'll let her have her way." Then he chuckled and added, "And I'll get the place cleaned up in the bargain."

Sure enough, the next day after the storm had passed, there would be the shanty solid as ever and clean as a whistle.

Other days I'd wander in just as Mr. Crosby was opening the big doors on the seaside to haul up burlap bags of shellfish. I'd watch the water stream from the bottoms of the bags.

When the bags were set down inside, the water would snake across the floor, search out the cracks, and fall back into the sea.

I'd slip off the stool and wriggle my toes in the riverlets. The water was so cold, I'd shiver, but I loved doing it anyway. No matter how warm the water was on the surface outside, I knew the iciness that existed at the bottom where the shellfish were kept.

The bags that had been brought in would snap and hiss for a while. I could picture quahog shells slapping shut and the clams pulling in their necks. I'd giggle, picturing them shutting themselves up like a bunch of turtles.

The men let them rest and relax a while, which made them easier to open.

When the weather turned cold, the stove in the corner would ping and smoke a little, giving enough warmth to make the shanty a welcoming place, especially to the men who had been out working on the bay. Grandpa would come in, his cheeks reddened from the cold. He'd slap his gloves together, then take them off and warm his fingers at the stove.

That done, he'd light his pipe, and muss my hair, pleased to see me. He'd talk with the others about the catch that day. Then we'd bundle up. He'd pick up his lunchbox and take my hand. We'd say goodbye and walk home.

Going to the shanty was always wonderful to me. Maybe it was that we kids could always count on Mr. Crosby to give us a bull quahog for bait to go fishing. He never chased us out. Maybe it was the pet seagull, "Oyster," who would come when called, swooping out of nowhere to take a morsel from my outstretched fingers. Perhaps it was because sometimes it made me feel my beginnings. The ocean smells seemed part of me.

Maybe it was a young girl's love for her grandfather that made the shanty so unforgettable.

It probably was all of these. Whatever it was, the shanty is one of the special places of my heart.

Robert Brooks did this pen
and ink sketch for me.
He certainly captured the
shanty of my childhood.

Adventures

Breaking In

The beautiful homes near the water in our village appeared like castles to us. They didn't have moats, but many of them had turrets and high widows walks, stained glass windows accenting odd shaped small rooms, jutting here and there on different sides and levels of the buildings.

In our imaginations, some of these rooms probably held captive princesses or witches walled up forever.

If and when we were sent to the houses to deliver something, we always went to the back door where we were met by a sinister looking housekeeper or harried looking maid who would take our package and whisk us away from the house quickly before we could see anything interesting.

After the houses were closed for the winter, we would sometimes ride on our bikes or walk in front on the beach looking for sand-glass and other treasures.

We were sure we could hear moans of despair coming from the turret rooms. Usually we convinced ourselves that it was just the wind but on other windless days we couldn't find any explanation for the eerie sounds that emanated from the abandoned structures.

Finally my friend, Judy, convinced me that we should investigate.

(She was into the Nancy Drew mysteries at the time.)

So here we were.

We weren't planning a crime. Our intentions were honorable.

We took off our shoes and brushed the bottom of our socks. When you're ten years old, there's no guarantee that your socks will be clean.

125

We slipped quietly into the back hall. Judy tried the kitchen door. It was latched but not locked.

We wouldn't have to go through a window. If we could just walk in, it wouldn't seem like we were doing a really bad thing.

We certainly didn't think of it as breaking and entering. In the first place we didn't have to break to enter.

We stepped into the kitchen. It was such a disappointment! It was plain and not nearly as pretty as my grandmother's, no colorful knickknacks on the windowsills or bright plates on the counters or walls. It cried out that it was strictly a place for working, not for quiet cups of tea and talk while preparing meals, not a place for a young girl to beg a cookie or two as they came out of the oven.

Beyond the kitchen was a small narrow room with a sink and counter, with cupboards above holding hundreds of glasses. We learned later that this was the butlers pantry.

It held little interest for us so we moved on.

When we got beyond the work areas, everything changed. A hall as wide as some of the rooms in our homes stretched before us. There was a beautiful thick carpet. Without further thought, we sat down and slipped off our socks. Sinking our bare feet into that silky thickness was wonderful, an opportunity not to be missed. I stretched my big toe off the edge of the carpet onto the wood floor. It was as smooth as it looked, like satin. I knew what satin felt like because my grandmother had a small satin cushion she cherished. She would let me hold it once in a while after I had carefully washed my hands.

With socks in hand, we advanced down the hall, coming next to the front foyer which boasted a wide staircase, swirling its way to the second floor.

We looked at each other and with silent but mutual consent, decided to save the upstairs for later.

The front hall led to many rooms, but through one door we could see a huge chandelier hanging over a table that must have had a dozen chairs around it.

126

Tiptoeing in we looked across the room to the French doors that took up most of the wall on the beach side.

We walked very carefully around the furniture, trying to drink in everything at once. I was so busy looking at the giant marble fireplace that I bumped into Judy causing her to knock into a table.

The lamp on it shivered a little as did I, but didn't fall.

"Be careful where you're going," snarled Judy. "If we break anything we'll probably end up in jail."

What a terrible thought! It took the wind out of our sails for a few minutes, but all the wonders we were seeing soon brought back our excitement.

After wandering through the living room and library, where we reverently touched some leather books and a world globe, we decided to brave the second floor.

After all, this had been our original purpose, to see what the turreted rooms held.

We crept silently up the circular staircase.

Although some of the windows were shuttered against the winter weather that would soon be coming, the sun managed to give the rooms a light and airy appearance, not frightening at all.

When we found the turreted room we were surprised to find it was like any other room except the turret gave it a small alcove with a window seat overlooking the sound.

We decided it was definitely a room for a captive princess, who sat at the window watching for her prince to come in a ship to rescue her.

Judy opened a closet door and there on a hook, beckoning us, was a beautiful hat, with a wide brim, wrapped in an enormous pink ribbon.

"I've got to try it on," I breathed.

"Okay," said Judy, "you first."

We took turns trying it on in front of the mirror that hung over an ornate bureau.

It was a hat fit for a princess and for an instant, each of us became one.

Finally, we knew it was time to go.

We hung the hat in its proper place, looked out at the sea to imagine a ship on the horizon.

We walked as elegantly as is possible with bare feet, down that beautiful staircase and into the kitchen, where slipping our socks back on, we turned once again into a couple of imaginative, adventurous, ten-year old girls.

The Great Bridge Adventure

In the early forties we spent a lot of time at the drawbridge which connects the village with Little Island. About one hundred feet across the channel is Little Island and Grand Island, now known as Oyster Harbors. The only way to the island is by boat or the drawbridge. It has to be a drawbridge because there are two boatyards on the village side. If a person wanted to go out on the sound to do some fishing or sail around the world, he would have to go under the bridge and out through the Cut, between the mainland and Dead Neck, a narrow strip of land.

The bridge attendant during the forties, was Mr. Dill. His job was to raise and lower the bridge when boat traffic made it necessary, and keep an eye on things in general. This included watching all of us children that congregated there most days.

When Mr. Dill heard three blasts of a horn, he would check out the boat coming through to see how high he had to raise the bridge, and to make sure it wasn't one of us kids playing tricks on him. Then he would come out of his office which was built on the side in the middle of the bridge and shut the gates at each end of the span to stop traffic to and from the island. Having done that, he'd raise the bridge.

After the boat had gone through, the pilot would wave, toot his horn and yell his thanks. The gates would then be put back in their standing positions. The boys often helped him with this.

The bridge was a great place to fish. Across the channel Johnny Crosby had an oyster shanty. He'd give each of us a bull quahog for bait, and off we'd go.

It was mostly boys there, but I tagged along with my brother, Earle, who was five years older. As long as I didn't act squeamish about things, I was usually left alone and not teased.

There were stairs down to a platform on one side of the bridge. From the platform, you could reach some concrete shelves which were part of the bridge structure. Both spots were ideal for fishing.

There was the usual rough-housing and pushing each other into the water, but nobody minded much. We all swam like fish.

Once in a while someone would catch a "Cape Cod Minister." They were ugly little fish, small and brightly colored, but vicious. It was impossible to get them off the line and they were exceptionally hard to kill. The boys would just cut their lines and curse about losing their hooks to those rotten things.

When they caught them, I would have to steel myself not to act afraid because if they'd had an inkling of how I felt, they would have chased me with one from there to kingdom come.

Sometimes we would jump off the bridge if Mr. Dill wasn't looking. It was pretty high, probably about fifteen feet, and of course higher at low tide. One day I jumped on a dare at low tide and hit the water with such force that I stuck fast in the mud. I struggled with all my might and finally shook loose, coughing and gagging as I broke the surface. I looked up to see my brother swimming frantically toward me. Of course, once he realized I was all right, he gave me a swat and informed me of how stupid I was.

Soon after that day, the boys found a new thrill. When Mr. Dill started raising the bridge, one of them would run up the road bed as it was going up. Grabbing onto the railing that was on the side, he would cling there until the bridge completed its rise. Then just as it started its descent, the boy would drop through the opening and be in the water long before the bridge mechanism clanged shut.

Mr. Dill really lit into them about this latest trick, but once he was in the act of raising the bridge, there wasn't much he could do about it and he wasn't in a position to see them when they started up.

The day that turned out to be the last day of my bridge life dawned sunny, warm and bright. I tagged after my brother, thinking what a great day for swimming and fishing.

When we arrived, the boys started teasing me about being a girl and scaredy cat. I knew something was up, but didn't know what. I soon found out! I was to do the trick.

My stomach lurches now at the thought of it even after all these years, but at the time, if I hadn't agreed to it my life would have been too miserable to endure.

We waited. I prayed for a small boat so the bridge wouldn't have to be raised very high, but it was not to be. One part of me wanted to get it over. I knew I was going to die and waiting around all day for it to happen wasn't that great.

Finally it came. "Toot, toot, toot." The boys all gathered around me, maybe to keep me from running away, which had certainly crossed my mind.

As the bridge began to rise, I ran up the grade and grabbed the railing at the end.

"I can't do this," I yelled, but even as I hollered, I knew it was too late to stop. When the bridge was completely raised, I looked down. It was so far to the water. As the bridge started coming down, the gang started shouting at me.

"Jump, hurry," they were all screaming.

I couldn't breathe and I couldn't let go.

Finally a voice penetrated my fear.

"Jump, you little fool," yelled my brother. "Jump or you'll be crushed."

I jumped.

A second later, the two sides of the bridge screeched when they meshed together. I plummeted down to the water one second ahead of disaster.

My bridge days were over!

This is what the bridge looked like the day I thought was my last.

The Theater

A short time ago, I was listening to a commercial on television offering a group of songs from the 40's, such as "I'll Walk Alone." Sad and lonely feelings welled up in me. I had been too young during the war to have been romantically involved with a serviceman so I think these feelings came from all the war movies we saw. The Osterville Community Theater had played a big part in our young lives.

The theater was located in the middle of the village next to the drugstore. I don't remember ever paying to see a movie until I was grown. The manager, Mr. Kunze, let us in free. We, in turn, put the covers back on the seats between showings. Because of this great system, we saw a lot of movies, many of them more than once. The war movies gave us ideas for our games. The songs imbued us with those feelings of loneliness, loss, and yearnings that are still brought forth today when hearing them.

There were happy endings in most of the shows and they would evoke feelings of patriotism and pride in being Americans. This pride created a lot of problems during play. We all wanted to be the "good guys." Nobody wanted to play the dreaded "Axis." Much of a Saturday morning could be involved in deciding that issue!

There were other movies that worked their magic on us. Technicolor was just coming into its own. We were thrilled when Dorothy landed in Oz and the world turned into color. We were also terrified by the *Picture of Dorian Gray*, when all that ghastly evil was thrust upon us in living color.

We were impressed by the fact that the inventor of this marvelous technique had a home two miles away in Centerville. Our local pride was reinforced every time we saw the name, Natalie Kalmus, in the credits. We would brag to each other that we'd been in her house or had seen her.

One afternoon at the end of the movie, my friend, Judy, and I discovered the door to the broom closet open and spied a ladder attached to the wall. We climbed to the second floor. The light was streaming in so we ventured into the room.

Tiptoeing around, we discovered a huge chandelier that had hung in the theater in another era. We oohed and aahed over it for several minutes. It was the most magnificent thing we'd ever seen. We were awed. Gradually our curiosity and desire to touch it overcame our fears of breaking it. We picked up some crystals that had become detached and turned them every which way, watching the colors dance magically around the room.

Gradually, the light began to fade as the sun went down. We finally realized how late it had become. It began to feel creepy up in this big old space with its shadowed corners.

We moved slowly toward the ladder. I don't remember who reached it first but I think we were so close to each other, we could have been glued together. At the bottom of the ladder, we found the closet was closed but not locked. We went out into the main part of the theater. It was empty and all the doors were secured.

We knew if we didn't arrive home soon, we'd be in big trouble. We had to get out.

The rear exit of the theater was close to the back of the drugstore. Beside the theater door was a small window, locked and shuttered. After searching every other way out, we decided that the little window was our only chance. We were able to open the window but had to break the shuttered part.

Squeezing out as quietly as possible, we hung for a moment and then dropped to the ground, hoping desperately that nobody would open the back door of the drugstore and catch us. All was quiet. We gave each other a V for victory sign and sped home.

The broken shutter caused a little stir in the village. Those who saw it commented that perhaps some of the bigger boys in town had tried to break in. Little did they know, it had been two small girls breaking out!

The Watchbug

I seem to have spent a lot of my childhood being afraid of one thing or another. Perhaps it was the time we grew up in.

People were more superstitious then.

Oh, I know we still throw salt over our shoulder when we spill it, and some of us avoid walking under ladders, but overall we are less intimidated by old wives tales than preceding generations.

The most frightening superstition I recall was the "watch bug." The watch bug is, in reality, a small beetle that lives in the walls of some old houses, but in my childhood it was considered much more than that.

The house I grew up in was about a hundred and fifty years old. It had all sorts of creaks and other noises. I was used to most of them, but one night when lying in my bed, I heard a new one.

Tick-tock, tick-tock. The sound came clearly. Something was behind the wall. How could a clock get in there? I thought about waking my parents, but thought better of it.

I kept listening to the ticking and finally fell asleep.

In the morning when I woke I immediately listened for the sound.

Nothing. Maybe I'd dreamed it.

Later I went into my great-grandmother's apartment.

"Grandma," I said, "I heard something ticking in the walls last night before I went to sleep. It sounded like a clock. I didn't hear it when I got up this morning."

"Oh, dear," she said, frowning. "It must have been a watch bug."

"A watch bug. What's a watch bug?"

" A watch bug ticking is fine, but when it stops," she paused.

"When it stops, what?" I asked.

"When it stops ticking, it means somebody's going to die," she answered.

"That's crazy," I said. Suddenly I was scared. "What's a bug got to do with someone dying?"

I laughed as though it was a joke.

"Laugh, if you want, young lady," she said, "but mark my words."

"Well, he's probably still ticking, anyway. He just crawled off to another part of the eaves where I couldn't hear him," I said hopefully.

Grandma looked at me and smiled. I guess she realized she'd scared me

"Pay me no mind, child. It's just an old wives tale."

That evening, a neighbor, Mrs. Parker, died. Oh, I know she was old and had been sick a while, but why'd she have to pick that particular time to move on?

The next morning before the school bell rang, the kids were standing around discussing, Mrs. Parker.

I piped up and said, "I knew something was going to happen. The watch bug told me."

Everyone stopped talking and looked at me.

"What are you talking about, you dope?" said Tom, who was two years ahead of me in school.

Tom really had it in for me since I gave him a bloody nose after he'd put a snake down my back. I hadn't meant to, but in flailing around, I managed to hit him right square on the nose. He'd had a hard time living it down.

Now, he laughed at me, "A watch bug! Whoever heard of a watch bug?" he scoffed.

"A watch bug lives in the walls of old houses and goes tick-tock tick-tock." I tick-tocked right in old Tom's face.

Then I turned to the others and said in a low dramatic voice, "Do you know what happens when he stops ticking?"

They all shook their heads, spellbound.

135

I fell to the ground and gurgled, "Somebody dies."

"No kidding!" "Wow!" "Where'd you hear that?"

Their reactions were everything I could have wanted. Even Tom was suitably impressed.

I told them all what I'd heard and what my great-grandmother had said. When I got to the end of the telling, they had no trouble making the connection with old Mrs. Parker.

We moved a little closer to each other, as if for protection against the doings of the adult world surrounding us.

As for me, spreading the fear around a little seemed to thin it out a bit, and the boys "tick-tocking" around school all that day diluted the fear even more, till by the end of the day there was more fun than fear.

Bedtime that night brought it all back though, and took my breath away as I lay under the covers waiting... but I heard nothing.

We were safe for now.

Hannah Screecham

Recently I read a variation of Osterville's Hannah Screecham legend. It reminded me of an incident in my childhood that took place one fall.

We grew up with stories of Hannah woven into our lives. One story was that Hannah was a companion of Captain Kidd, the pirate. She came ashore on Grand Island with him each time he buried treasure. He would shoot the men who buried it so that they couldn't tell anyone about its location. Finally, he became suspicious of Hannah and shot her, too. Ever since then, her ghost supposedly guards the treasures and screams wildly if anyone comes near. Most people run away when they hear her, but if they don't... doom.

Sightings were frequent and reported with relish. My grandfather, William Hodges, wrote and published his own "Legend of Hannah Screecham."

He would regale us with stories of Hannah. These he told with a twinkle in his eye, to let us know that they shouldn't be taken too seriously.

It was in the early forties, when there was an old wooden water tower on Oyster Harbors. My brother, took me along this day to the tower where he and his friends liked to play their war games.

It was decided that I was to be the lookout in the tower. I thought at the time, it was a pretty important part. It was only much later that I realized they were just getting me out of the way.

As late afternoon passed, the sun seemed to drop like a stone into the bay. We became aware of the long shadows disappearing into the dusk.

Supper time.

Everyone drifted towards home, everyone except me, that is. My brother turned to see where I was. He looked around, then up. There I was frozen at the top of the ladder.

He hollered for me to hurry up.

This I couldn't do. I wanted to hurry. I wanted desperately to move, but could not. When he realized I wasn't coming, he signaled to his friends to keep going.

He stood at the bottom of the ladder and yelled at me to come down.

"I can't. I'm afraid," I whimpered.

For the next half hour, as night moved in around the tower, he threatened, cajoled, and finally begged me to descend.

At that time, I was more afraid of the ladder, than my brother.

Finally, his patience snapped and he informed me in a cold voice that he was leaving and I could stay there all night as far as he was concerned.

After delivering this speech, he started to walk off, flinging the ultimate threat over his shoulder.

"I hope SHE gets you."

He didn't need to name her. I knew he meant Hannah Screecham. We were right in her territory.

My options were few; climbing down those rickety stairs, falling to certain death; braving my brother's anger at being embarrassed in front of his friends; or being left at the mercy of Hannah.

It was decided for me when a terrible screech bit into the night, echoing in the darkness. I was down those rungs in two seconds flat, and racing toward my brother.

He grabbed my hand and dragged me after him through bush and briar, pausing for nothing until we crossed the Oyster Harbors bridge.

We flopped to the ground, exhausted and trembling.

In a few minutes when we were able to breathe once more, I asked him. "Do you think it was really HER?"

"Nah," he replied in a jagged voice, "probably just an old screech owl or some other critter."

We looked at each other steadily for a few seconds.

I knew we were making a trade-off.

I wouldn't tell his friends how scared he had been and he wouldn't pummel me for embarrassing him in front of them.

He stood up.

"Let's go home," he said.

102 Chickens

It all started when my mother allowed that I could celebrate my ninth birthday with a party.

My friend, Paul arrived at the appointed time with a gaily wrapped present.

Three fluffy, yellow baby chicks peeped at me as I lifted the lid.

Who has never loved a baby chick? Soft, round, cuddly.

The small quiet one I named Sleepy. If I'd only known!

The other two chicks names have been long forgotten, but not Sleepy.

He grew up to be my own personal nightmare, a fierce, rotten tempered rooster who bullied anyone who came near. Tyrant emperor of the hen yard.

Cuddling him at my party, I had no inkling of what was to come.

Our family was enchanted with the chicks.

My parents explored all possibilities. We could have fresh eggs and fried chicken dinners. We could sell the extra eggs. That would more than pay for feed. Of course they realized we couldn't do all this with three chicks. We need a few more.

Dad ordered one hundred day old chicks from Sears and Roebucks.

He built a small chicken coop and yard. Before the chicks arrived, we were told to plan on about one fourth of them living. That would be just right my dad thought. Twenty-five plus my three, a nice flock.

Ninety-nine survived! We now had one hundred two chickens. Dad had to double the size of the hen house and yard.

Baby chicks are one thing, chickens are another.

Although I claimed ownership of only three of these creatures, I was appointed to feed and pick up eggs.

Nasty job! How I hated it!

I tried being nice. "Here, chick, chick, chick," I'd call pleasantly as I tossed the feed to the clucking hens. All was well until I'd draw Sleepy's attention. The remaining feed was usually thrown directly at this king of the yard to slow him down as he chased me from his domain.

I had to pick up the eggs and get out before he caught me, so I'd wait outside the yard until he was busy strutting around, showing off for his harem. Then I'd slip into the hen house and shut the door before he realized I'd come through the yard. Getting out was the problem.

The trick was to dash through the squawking hens before he could catch and peck me.

Sometimes I made it, sometimes I didn't.

Sometimes the eggs didn't make it either, and I'd be in trouble.

Finally, after several months, my mother grew tired of listening to me moaning and groaning about having to gather eggs. I'd long since given up going in the yard to feed. I just threw the stuff over the fence and put their water tub where I could fill it from outside.

She decided that although she thought I was making much ado about nothing, she would take over that chore while I took another.

I followed her out the first time she went to collect eggs. She walked into the yard. Sleepy charged her. She snapped her apron at him. He stopped in his tracks. She collected the eggs without incident.

This went on for several days. Then it happened. After picking up the eggs, Mother walked nonchalantly toward the gate.

He came from nowhere. He flew at her back and nearly knocked her to the ground. The eggs went flying. She fought him off with the egg basket while fleeing for the gate where I was yelling at her and the rooster. When the gate was locked and she was safely on the outside, I could see she was bleeding from one finger where he had pecked her. She carried the scar from that encounter for the rest of her life. As for Sleepy, his days were numbered.

Meanwhile, the fried chicken dinners we had anticipated were preceded by such unappetizing activities that I didn't care about eating the final result.

My father and brother killed and dressed the chickens, performing their grisly ritual at a chopping block at the rear of the house. My brother held the chicken while Dad chopped its head off. If I happened to be in the vicinity, this was followed by my brother chasing me around the yard with the chicken's head.

Next, my mother would put the chicken in a pot of boiling water to loosen the feathers so they could be plucked. While this was going on, a terrible smell permeated the kitchen. This whole procedure was enough to turn a person's stomach against chicken forever.

The first year or so, it was wonderful to have so many eggs, but gradually the thrill wore off, like everything else connected with those birds. It seemed like we had eggs in some form most meals. Omelets, egg salad sandwiches, eggnogs, custards...you name it.

Finally, we'd had enough, so my dad sold the rest of the flock.

"Never again," said my father. We all bobbed our heads in agreement.

A month later, Dad brought home a pair of white mice in a small cage. Soon another large cage was bustling with them. Then came the day the ones in the big cage got loose in the house.

But that's another story.